A Calendar of Wisdom

DAILY THOUGHTS TO NOURISH THE SOUL
WRITTEN AND SELECTED FROM THE
WORLD'S SACRED TEXTS BY

LEO TOLSTOY

TRANSLATED FROM THE RUSSIAN BY

PETER SEKIRIN

SCRIBNER

This translation is dedicated to
MELISSA TEMERTY

SCRIBNER
1230 Avenue of the Americas
New York, NY 10020

Introduction, translation, and compilation
copyright © 1997 by Peter Sekirin

SCRIBNER and design are trademarks of Simon & Schuster Inc.

DESIGNED BY ERICH HOBBING

Set in Stempel Garamond

Manufactured in the United States of America

7   9   10   8

Library of Congress Cataloging-in-Publication Data

Tolstoy, Leo, graf, 1828–1910.
[Krug chteniia. English. Selections]
A calendar of wisdom : daily thoughts to nourish the soul / written and
selected from the world's sacred texts by Leo Tolstoy; translated from the
Russian by Peter Sekirin.
p. cm.
This translation, drawn from the enl. and completely rev. second ed., does
not include the fifty-two stories called "The Sunday reading stories."
Includes index.
(alk. paper)
1. Conduct of life—Quotations, maxims, etc. I. Sekirin, Peter.
II. Title.
BJ1581.2.T626213   1997
087'.1—dc21   97-23501
CIP

ISBN 0-684-83793-5

TRANSLATOR'S
ACKNOWLEDGMENTS

I would like to express my deepest and most sincere acknowledgments to the following people:

professors who introduced me to Russian literature: K. Lantz, R. Bogert, Ch. Barnes, H. Marshall, R. Lindheim, O. Bakitsh, C. Bedford, M. Valdez, L. Hutcheon; and other professors and students of the Slavic Department and the Department of Comparitive Literature of the University of Toronto;

my literary agent, Ivy Fischer Stone, of the Fifi Oscard Agency;

my friend Kim Yates and Stella Cho, who read the manuscript;

my parents, Vera and Vsevolod Sekirin;

the staff at Scribner, especially my editor Scott Moyers and Susan Moldow;

Their wisdom and tireless support have helped this project to become a reality.

—PETER SEKIRIN, Toronto 1996

TOLSTOY AND THE CREATION OF *A Calendar of Wisdom*

PETER SEKIRIN

This was Leo Tolstoy's last major work. With it, he fulfilled a dream he had nourished for almost fifteen years, that of "collecting the wisdom of the centuries in one book" meant for a general audience. Tolstoy put a huge amount of effort into its creation, preparing three revised editions between 1904 and 1910. It was his own favorite everyday reading, a book he would turn to regularly for the rest of his life.

The original idea for this work appeared to come to Tolstoy in the mid-1880s. His first recorded expression of the concept of *A Calendar of Wisdom*—"A wise thought for every day of the year, from the greatest philosophers of all times and all people"—came in 1884. He wrote in his diary on March 15 of that year: "I have to create a circle of reading for myself: Epictetus, Marcus Aurelius, Lao-Tzu, Buddha, Pascal, The New Testament. This is also necessary for all people." In 1885, he wrote in a letter to his assistant, Mr. Chertkov: "I know that it gives one great inner force, calmness, and happiness to communicate with such great thinkers as Socrates, Epictetus, Arnold, Parker.... They tell us about what is most important for humanity, about the meaning of life and about virtue. . . . I would like to create a book . . . in which I could tell a person about his life, and about the Good Way of Life."

The process of collecting these thoughts took over fifteen years. Tolstoy began writing between December 1902 and January 1903. Then in his late seventies, he had fallen seriously ill; while meditating about the meaning of life and death, he was inspired to begin compiling what he then called *A Wise Thought for Every Day*. When he finally sent the book to his publisher, Tolstoy wrote in his diary: "I felt that I have been elevated to great spiritual and moral heights by communication with the best and wisest people whose books I read and whose thoughts I selected for my *Circle of Reading*." He would often return in his diary to meditate upon this book, repeating variants of "What can be more precious than to communicate every day with the wisest men of the world?" Tolstoy carefully selected the contributors to this volume, "among the very best writers," as he repeated to his colleagues and friends. They represented a wide variety of philosophical views, cultural backgrounds, and historical periods: "It will be a big surprise to the readers," Tolstoy wrote, "that together with Kant and other famous thinkers, they will find in my book thoughts by Lucy Malory, an unknown journalist from the United States, from Oregon." The first edition appeared in 1904 under the title *Thoughts of Wise Men*. It saw three editions during Tolstoy's lifetime, between 1904 and 1910, each published with a different subtitle: *The Way of Life*, *Circle of Reading*, and *A Wise Thought for Every Day*.

Between 1904 and 1907, Tolstoy worked on the enlarged and completely revised second edition, from which this, its first English translation, is drawn. In mid-August 1905 he wrote the introduction that follows and noted in his diary: "I have revised and enlarged my *Calendar*, now it is twice as big. For two months I did not read anything else, neither newspapers nor magazines, and I felt so good. . . . I became more and more astonished by the ignorance, and especially by the cultural, moral ignorance of our society. . . . All our education should be directed to the accumulation of the cultural heritage of our ancestors, the best thinkers of the world."

The major difference between the first edition (*Thoughts of Wise Men*) and the second (*A Calendar of Wisdom*) was that Tolstoy now grouped the thoughts according to topics for a certain day, week, and month. He wrote on June 3, 1904, in his diary: "I am busy with the *Circle of Reading*. . . . I cannot do anything else. . . . I have selected thoughts and grouped them into the following major topics: God, Intellect, Law, Love, Divine Nature of Mankind, Faith, Temptations, Word, Self-Sacrifice, Eternity, Good, Kindness, Unification of People (with God), Prayer, Freedom, Perfection, Work, etc." Tolstoy added about eight hundred of his own thoughts, written during his many years of meditation, or taken from previous diary entries. He generally started each day with an opening thought of his own, added quotes by other sources, and finished each day with a closing thought of his own.

Additionally, he wrote a short story, or vignette, three to ten pages in length for the end of every week. Each story corresponded to that week's moral, philosophical, or religious topic; he prepared fifty-two stories in all and called them *The Sunday Reading Stories.* The majority of these fifty-two stories were written by Tolstoy especially for this work; the rest were selected and adapted from writings by Plato, Buddha, Dostoevski, Pascal, Leskov, Chekhov, and others. Tolstoy's prose style in these *Sunday Reading Stories* is very different from the sophistication of his earlier novels. These stories, which were later greatly admired by Pasternak and Solzhenitsyn, were written in a clear, simple, almost primitive language, designed, as they were, for a wide and general audience. In them, Tolstoy combined simplicity of form and philosophical depth. Because these stories did not appear in all editions, and because they are as a whole quite long, they do not appear in this edition.

On December 21, 1904, after reading the galley proofs of the second edition called *The Calendar: The Circle of Reading for Every Day,* Tolstoy wrote in his diary: "During this last day I have descended from the spiritual and moral heights where I was all this time when I communicated with the best and wisest thinkers of the world when I created my *Circle of Reading.*" This title was changed in the second revised edition, published in 1905–1907, to *Wise Thoughts by Many Writers on Truth, Life, and Behavior Collected and Arranged for Every Day of the Year by Leo Tolstoy.* From its first publication, the book was always present on Tolstoy's desk; it became his favorite book during the last five years of his life. Every day, from 1905 to 1910, he read thoughts presented in the book for the corresponding day of the year, and he recommended the same habit to all his friends. On May 16, 1908, he wrote to a man named Gusev: "I cannot understand how some people can live without communicating with the wisest people who ever lived on Earth? . . . I feel very happy every day, because I read this book."

Tolstoy prepared a third revised, shortened, and simplified edition which appeared in print under the new title *The Way of Life* in 1910, the last year of his life. He wished to make the book easily comprehensible for even the simplest and least educated people—peasants and children. Most probably, Tolstoy compared *A Calendar of Wisdom* to *War and Peace* when he wrote that "To create a book for the masses, for millions of people . . . is incomparably more important and fruitful than to compose a novel of the kind which diverts some members of the wealthy classes for a short time, and then is forever forgotten. The region of this art of the simplest, most widely accessible feeling is enormous, and it is as yet almost untouched." Other editions appeared in Odessa and St. Petersburg in 1911–1912. A German critical edition (translated by E. Schmidt and A. Schkarvan, Dresden: Karl Reissner, 1907) included the sources of his numerous quotes.

An edition of *A Calendar of Wisdom* was published in Russia in 1912, but after the Russian Revolution publication was forbidden under the Soviet regime, because of the book's spiritual orientation and its numerous religious quotes. When it was again published in Russia, in 1995, after the recent democratic reforms, it enjoyed tremendous success, selling over 300,000 copies.

It has never before been translated into English. The first English translation of *A Calendar of Wisdom* will be a real discovery for the English-speaking reader. Created by one of the world's greatest novelists and thinkers to represent the very best of the world's spiritual heritage, it draws on the greatest works of religion, philosophy, and literature the world has yet seen. It belongs among the very best creations of human genius, a work which will serve its readers as a practical spiritual guide on how to live in peace with oneself and how to live a life filled with kindness, satisfaction, and happiness. Tolstoy's original goal was the delivery of wisdom to the widest possible number of people, "to entertain millions of readers." This aim remains as compelling now, in this time of increasing spiritual need, as it was then.

INTRODUCTION

BY LEO TOLSTOY

I took the thoughts collected here from a very large number of works and collections. I indicated the author of each thought beneath it, though I did not mark the exact source or book title or work from which I took it. In some cases, I translated these thoughts not directly from their original sources, but from a translation from the languages in which they became known to me, so sometimes my translations might not be completely identical to the originals. When I translated thoughts by German, French, or Italian thinkers, I did not strictly follow the original, usually making it shorter and easier to understand, and omitting some words. Readers might tell me that a quote is not then Pascal or Rousseau, but my own work, but I think that there is nothing wrong in conveying their thoughts in a modified form. Therefore, if someone desires to translate this book into other languages, I would like to advise them not to look for the original quotes from the English poet Coleridge, say, or the German philosopher Kant, or the French writer Rousseau, but to translate directly from my writing. Another reason some of these thoughts may not correspond to the originals is at times I took a thought from a lengthy and convoluted argument, and I had to change some words and phrases for clarity and unity of expression. In some cases I even express the thought entirely in my own words. I did this because the purpose of my book is not to give exact, word-for-word translations of thoughts created by other authors, but to use the great and fruitful intellectual heritage created by different writers to present for a wide reading audience an easily accessible, everyday circle of reading which will arouse their best thoughts and feelings.

I hope that the readers of this book may experience the same benevolent and elevating feeling which I have experienced when I was working on its creation, and which I experience again and again, when I reread it every day, working on the enlargement and improvement of the previous edition.

—Leo Tolstoy, March 1908

Note to Reader: In all of the book's original Russian-language editions, Tolstoy highlighted on each page the one quote that most succinctly expressed the day's theme. These quotes have been italicized in this edition.

—Peter Sekirin

January 1

Better to know a few things which are good and necessary than many things which are useless and mediocre.

What a great treasure can be hidden in a small, selected library! A company of the wisest and the most deserving people from all the civilized countries of the world, for thousands of years, can make the results of their studies and their wisdom available to us. The thought which they might not even reveal to their best friends is written here in clear words for us, people from another century. Yes, we should be grateful for the best books, for the best spiritual achievements in our lives.

—RALPH WALDO EMERSON

There are too many mediocre books which exist just to entertain your mind. Therefore, read only those books which are accepted without doubt as good.

—LUCIUS ANNAEUS SENECA

Read the best books first, otherwise you'll find you do not have time.

—HENRY DAVID THOREAU

The difference between real material poison and intellectual poison is that most material poison is disgusting to the taste, but intellectual poison, which takes the form of cheap newspapers or bad books, can unfortunately sometimes be attractive.

January 2

One of the worst prejudices known is held by the majority of the so-called scholars of our time, who claim that a person can live without faith.

Throughout the centuries, in every age, people have wanted to know or at least have a vague idea about the source, the beginning, and the final purpose of their existence. Religion satisfies this requirement, and makes clear those connections which unite all people as brothers, revealing to them that they have the same source of origin, the same task for their lives, and the same general final goal.

—GIUSEPPE MAZZINI

The essential meaning of every religion is to answer the question "Why do I live, and what is my attitude to the limitless world which surrounds me?" There is not a single religion, from the most sophisticated to the most primitive, which does not have as its basis the definition of this attitude of a person to the world.

At the heart of all religions lies a single unifying truth. Let Persians bear their taovids, Jews wear their caps, Christians bear their cross, Muslims bear their sickle moon, but we have to remember that these are all only outer signs. The general essence of all religions is love to your neighbor, and that this is requested by Manuf, Zoroaster, Buddha, Moses, Socrates, Jesus, Saint Paul, and Mohammed alike.

—EWALD FLÜGEL

The life of a person without faith is the life of an animal.

January 3

Those who know the rules of true wisdom are baser than those who love them. Those who love them are baser than those who follow them.

—CHINESE PROVERB

The most important question to keep before ourselves at all times is this: Do we do the right thing? During this short period of time which we call our life, do our acts conform to the will of the force that sent us into the world? Do we do the right thing?

When I am in difficult circumstances, I ask God to help me. But it is my duty to serve the Lord, and not His to serve me. As soon as I remember this, my burden becomes lighter.

We have to fulfill honestly and irreproachably the work destined for us. It does not matter whether we hope that we will become angels some day, or believe that we have originated from slugs.

—JOHN RUSKIN

Just imagine that the purpose of your life is your happiness only—then life becomes a cruel and senseless thing. You have to embrace what the wisdom of humanity, your intellect, and your heart tell you: that the meaning of life is to serve the force that sent you into the world. Then life becomes a constant joy.

January 4

Even if we don't want to, we can't help but feel our connection to the rest of mankind: we are connected by industry, by trade, by art, by knowledge, and most importantly, by our common mortality.

Kind people help each other even without noticing that they are doing so, and evil people act against each other on purpose.

—CHINESE PROVERB

Every person has his burden. One cannot live without the support of other people; therefore we have to support each other with consolation, advice, and mutual warnings.

—From the BOOK OF DIVINE THOUGHTS

All the children of Adam are members of the same body. When one member suffers, all the others suffer as well. If you are indifferent to the sufferings of others, you do not deserve to be called a man.

—MUSLIH-UD-DIN SAADI

The history of mankind is the movement of humanity toward greater and greater unification.

January 5

Sometimes, the damage done by our words is obvious and sometimes it isn't, but the damage is not any smaller for our not being able to see those people who suffer from our words.

A gunshot wound may be cured, but the wound made by a tongue never heals.

—PERSIAN WISDOM

If any man offend not in word, the same is a perfect man.... Even so the tongue is a little member, and boasteth great things. Behold, how great a matter a little fire kindleth!

—JAMES 3:2, 5

When you hear people speak about the viciousness of other people, do not share in pleasure by discussing these issues. When you hear about the bad deeds of people, do not listen to the end and try to forget what you have heard. When you hear about the virtues of other people, remember them and tell them to others.

—EASTERN WISDOM

Do listen to disputes, but be not so involved in disputes yourself.

—NIKOLAI GOGOL

I said, I will take heed to my ways, that I sin not with my tongue.

—PSALMS 39:1

Be afraid to destroy the unity of people by stirring bad feelings amongst them against another with your words.

It's important to strive to do good, and even more important to strive to abstain from evil.

Abstention should be a habit in your life; it should support you in your virtues. For he who is resolute in goodness, there is nothing that he could not overcome.

—LAO-TZU

Put at least half of your energy into making yourself free of empty wishes, and very soon you will see that in so doing you will receive much greater fulfillment and happiness.

—After EPICTETUS

God tests everyone, one with wealth, another with poverty. A rich man is tested in whether he would extend an arm of support to those who need it; a poor man in whether he would bear all his sufferings without discontent and with obedience.

—The TALMUD

I will call the right groom he who can stop his rage, which goes as fast as the fastest chariot. Other people have no power; they just hold the reins.

—DHAMMAPADA, a book of BUDDHIST WISDOM

No matter how many times you aim to achieve victory over your passions, do not give up. Every effort weakens the power of passion and makes it easier to gain victory over it.

Kindness is necessary in relationships with people. If you are not kind to a person, you are not fulfilling your major obligation.

You have to respect every person, no matter how miserable or ridiculous he or she may be. You should remember that in every person lives the same spirit which lives in us.

—After ARTHUR SCHOPENHAUER

Do not be cruel of heart to those who are tempted, but try to console them, just as you would like to be comforted.

—From the BOOK OF DIVINE THOUGHTS

(1) Do not postpone for tomorrow what you can do today. (2) Do not force another person to do what you can do by yourself. (3) Pride costs more than all that is necessary for food, drink, shelter, or dress. (4) We suffer so much, thinking about what could have happened, but not about what has actually happened. (5) If you lose your temper, count up to ten before you do or say anything. If you haven't calmed down, then count to a hundred; and if you have not calmed down after this, count up to a thousand.

—After THOMAS JEFFERSON

The kinder and the more thoughtful a person is, the more kindness he can find in other people.

Kindness enriches our life; with kindness mysterious things become clear, difficult things become easy, and dull things become cheerful.

January 8

Christian teaching is so simple that even small children can understand its meaning. Those people cannot understand it, and only those, who want to seem and to be called Christians without being real Christians.

Buddha said, "A man who starts to live for his soul is like a man who brings a lantern into a dark house. The darkness disappears at once. You have to be persistent in this, and your soul will have this light."

Christ expressed all His teachings in His last commandment: "Love each other, as I loved you. Everyone will see that you are my disciples, if you love each other." He did not say, "If you believe," but "If you love." Faith can change with time, because our knowledge is constantly changing. Love, on the contrary, never changes; love is eternal.

My religion is love to all living beings.

In order to fulfill Christianity, we have to destroy its perversions and restore its purity.

January 9

Knowledge is real knowledge only when it is acquired by the efforts of your intellect, not by memory.

Only when we forget what we were taught do we start to have real knowledge.
—HENRY DAVID THOREAU

A constant flow of thoughts expressed by other people can stop and deaden your own thought and your own initiative. . . . That is why constant learning softens your brain. . . . Stopping the creation of your own thoughts to give room for the thoughts from other books reminds me of Shakespeare's remark about his contemporaries who sold their land in order to see other countries.
—ARTHUR SCHOPENHAUER

A thought can advance your life in the right direction only when it answers questions which were asked by your soul. A thought which was first borrowed from someone else and then accepted by your mind and memory does not really much influence your life, and sometimes leads you in the wrong direction.

Read less, study less, but think more. Learn, both from your teachers and from the books which you read, only those things which you really need and which you really want to know.

January 10

The basis of all education is the establishment of our relationship to the beginning of all things, and the conclusions about our behavior which may be drawn from this.

But whosoever shall offend one of these little ones who believe in me, it were better for him that a millstone were hanged about his neck, and that he were drowned in the depth of the sea.

—MATTHEW 18:6–7

As we bring up our children, we have to remember that we are caretakers of the future. By improving their education, we improve the future of mankind, the future of this world.

—After IMMANUEL KANT

I think that the major obligation of parents and educators is to give children an understanding of the divine beginning that exists within them.

—WILLIAM ELLERY CHANNING

Religious upbringing is the basis of all education.

January 11

Perfection is impossible without humility. "Why should I strive for perfection, if I am already good enough?"

The higher the position you occupy among other people, the more humble you should be. Many people live in height and glory, but the mysteries of this world can be revealed only to those who are humble. Do not seek out complication. Treat your duty with respect. Do not study what you should not. More things have already been revealed to you than you can understand.

—From APOCRYPHA

The Son of man came not to be ministered unto, but to minister, and to give his life as ransom for many.

—MATTHEW 20:28

Some of your friends praise you, and others blame and criticize you; be closer to those who blame you and further from those who praise you.

—The TALMUD

When an arrow does not hit its target, the marksman blames himself, not another person. A wise man behaves in the same way.

—CONFUCIUS

Remember all the bad things which you have done, and try to avoid doing bad things again. Remembering only your good deeds will interfere with your doing good in the future.

There are people who take responsibility for making decisions for others and determining their relationship to God and to the world; and there are people, the overwhelming majority of them, who give this authority to the others, and blindly believe in everything they are told. Both groups of people commit an equal crime.

We are all like children who first repeat the unquestionable "truth" told to us by our grandmothers, then the "truth" told to us by our teachers, and then, when we become older, the "truth" told to us by prominent people.
—After RALPH WALDO EMERSON

Beware of false prophets, which come to you in sheep's clothing, but inwardly they are ravening wolves. Ye shall know them by their fruits. Do men gather grapes of thorns, or figs of thistles? Even so every good tree bringeth forth good fruit; but a corrupt tree bringeth forth evil fruit. A good tree cannot bring forth evil fruit, neither can a corrupt tree bring forth good fruit. Every tree that bringeth not forth good fruit is hewn down, and cast into the fire. Wherefore by their fruits ye shall know them.
—MATTHEW 7:15–20

A man should use that spiritual heritage which he has received from the wise and holy people of the past, but he should test everything with his intellect, accepting certain things and rejecting others.

Every person should define for himself his attitude to this world and to God.

Faith is the understanding of the meaning of life and the acceptance of those duties and responsibilities connected to it.

Who is a good man? Only a man who has faith is good. What is faith? This is when your will is in consent with the world's conscience and the world's wisdom.

—CHINESE PROVERB

We should do only one thing: give ourselves into the hands of God, whatever our ultimate fate. Allow that which should happen to happen. What will happen will be good.

—HENRY AMIEL

They say that Judgment Day will come and that God will be furious. But a good God cannot bring anything but good. Do not be afraid: the end will be full of joy.

—PERSIAN WISDOM

You should not worry too much about what will happen after death. Deliver yourself to the divine creature and bless it: you know that it is love, therefore, why should you be afraid?

When Christ died, he said, "Father! I deliver my spirit into Thy hands." Those who say these words, not with their tongue but with all their heart, do not need anything else. If my spirit returns back to its Father, this is the best place for it, and nothing can be better.

Don't think that you can find peace for your soul without faith.

You should love only one thing in yourself, that which is the same in all of us. In loving that which is the same in all of us, you love God.

Master, which is the great commandment in the law? Jesus said until him, Thou shalt love the Lord thy God with all thy heart, and with all thy soul, and with all thy mind. This is the first and great commandment. And the second is like unto it, Thou shalt love thy neighbor as thyself. On these two commandments hang all the law and the prophets.

—MATTHEW 22:36–40

People live by love: love of yourself is the beginning of death; love of other people and of God is the beginning of life.

God is love. And he who lives in love, lives in God, and God lives in him. If we love one another, God lives in us.

—I JOHN, from Chapter 4

Love is not a source, it is a consequence of our understanding the divine, spiritual beginning which exists in all of us.

January 15

The greatest truth of the teachings of Christ is the direct connection between a man (God's son) and God (His Father).

You ask me, what the most important feature of Christ's character was. I will answer you: it was his confidence in the greatness of the human soul. He saw in a person the reflection of God's image, and, therefore, he loved everyone, whoever a person was, without regard to his life or character.

—After WILLIAM ELLERY CHANNING

Both people and nations must get rid of prejudices. Feel yourself talking directly to God: don't read the book, read your soul; then a small chapel will become as big as the heavenly dome itself.

—After RALPH WALDO EMERSON

There are two ways of understanding God: either intellectually or spiritually, based on faith and morality. The intellectual understanding of God is not resolute enough and can be subjected to dangerous mistakes; spiritual understanding of God requires moral actions. This faith is both natural and supernatural.

—After IMMANUEL KANT

Beware of everything which puts an obstacle between you and God.

January 16

False faith is the major cause of most of our misfortunes.

The purpose of a human life is to bring the irrational beginning of our life to a rational beginning. In order to succeed in this, two things are important: (1) to see all irrational, unwise things in life and direct your attention to them and study them; (2) to understand the possibility of a rational, wise life. The major purpose of all teachers of mankind was the understanding of the irrational and rational beginnings in our life.

We should be ready to change our views at any time, and slough off prejudices, and live with an open and receptive mind. A sailor who sets the same sails all the time, without making changes when the wind changes, will never reach his harbor.

—HENRY GEORGE

Accept the teaching of Christ as it is, clear and simple; then you will see that we live among big lies.

Live for your soul, and without trying or even understanding that you're doing it, you will contribute to the
improvement of society.

Why do you torture yourself? You want kindness, but
you do not know where to find it. Know that you cannot
achieve anything without God.... God is your only Lord,
your only master, and you do not need another. God will
make you free.

—F. ROBERT DE LAMENNAIS

It would be nice if wisdom had such a quality that it could
flow from one man who is full of wisdom to another man
who has no wisdom, just as with two connected vessels
water flows from one vessel to the other until the water
level is the same in both of them. The problem is that to
obtain wisdom, you must make an independent, serious
effort of your own.

*If you can teach a person kindness and love, but you do not,
you lose a brother.*

—CHINESE PROVERB

Improve your own soul, and be confident that only in so
doing can you contribute to the improvement of the
larger society of which you are part.

January 18

A scholar knows many books; a well-educated person has knowledge and skills; an enlightened person understands the meaning and purpose of his life.

There are a limitless number of different sciences, but without one basic science, that is, what is the meaning of life and what is good for the people, all other forms of knowledge and art become idle and harmful entertainment.

We live a senseless life, contrary to the understanding of life by the wisest people of all times. This happens because our young generations are educated in the wrong way—they are taught different sciences but they are not taught the meaning of life.

The only real science is the knowledge of how a person should live his life. And this knowledge is open to everyone.

Society can be improved only by self-sacrifice.

Heaven and earth are eternal. They are eternal because they do not exist for themselves. In the same way, a truly holy person does not live for himself, and therefore he can become eternal, and can achieve anything.

—LAO-TZU

There is only one law, both in your personal and social life: if you want to improve your soul, you should be ready to sacrifice it.

The improvement of man can be measured by the level of his inner freedom. The more a person becomes free from his personality, the more freedom he has.

January 20

Death and birth are two limits, and something similar is hidden behind each.

When you think about what will happen to your soul after death, think also about what happened to your soul before your birth. If you plan to go somewhere, then you came from somewhere.

Where do we go after death? We go to where we came from. There is nothing which can be called ourselves in that land; therefore, we do not remember what has happened to us there.

When a person leads a good life, he is happy at the present moment and he does not think what will happen after this life. If he thinks of death, he looks at how well this life is laid out, and he believes that after death everything will be as good as it is now. It is much better to believe that everything which God makes for us is good than to believe in all the pleasures of paradise.

When we die, our souls become free.

—After HERACLITUS

A person should not think too much about what will happen after his life. Follow the will of those who sent us into this world; that will is in our minds and our hearts.

The more closely a person follows his intellect and controls his passions, the closer he comes to spiritual life, to love of God and of his neighbor.

We would think a man insane who, instead of covering his house with a roof and putting windows in his window frames, goes out in stormy weather, and scolds the wind, the rain, and the clouds. But we all do the same when we scold and blame the evil in other people instead of fighting the evil which exists in us. It is possible to get rid of the evil inside of us, as it is possible to make a roof and windows for our house. This is possible. But it is not possible for us to destroy evil in this world, just as we cannot order the weather to change and the clouds to disappear. If, instead of teaching others, we would educate and improve ourselves, then there would be less evil in this world, and all people would live better lives.

Do not be embarrassed by your mistakes. Nothing can teach us better than our understanding of them. This is one of the best ways of self-education.

—THOMAS CARLYLE

It seems to us that the most important work in the world is the work which is visible, which we can see: building a house, plowing the land, feeding cattle, gathering fruits; and that the work which is invisible, the work done by our soul, is not important. But our invisible work at the improvement of our soul is the most important work in the world, and all other visible kinds of work are useful only when we do this major work.

No exceptions or special circumstances can justify the murder of a living person. Murder is the most vulgar violation of the Law of God as it is expressed in all religious teachings and in all people's conscience.

Military service makes people corrupt, because the military, in time of peace, abides in complete idleness; they lack any useful labor, they are freed of the obligations of such work. Instead, they create notions of honor of regiment, or of banner, or the complete subjugation of one person by another.

When civilians get into these circumstances, they become ashamed of such a way of life. The military, on the contrary, are proud of it and boast of this way of life, especially during periods of war. They say: "We are ready to risk our lives at war, and therefore such a careless joyful life is necessary for us, and we have the right to lead it."

The same divine beginning lives in all people, and no single person or gathering of people has the right to destroy this connection between the divine beginning and a human body, that is, to take a human life.

January 23

Among all sins, there is one which completely opposes the major blessing of human life, which is your love for your brother: there is no worse sin than to destroy this major joy of life, by feeling rage and hatred for your brother.

Seneca, a wise man from Rome, said that when you want to escape from your rage, when you feel that it grows, the best thing to do is to stop. Do not do anything: do not walk, do not move, do not speak. If your body or your tongue moves at this moment, then your rage will grow.

Rage is very harmful for all people, but it is most harmful for the man who experiences it.

An evil person damages not only others but himself.
—After SOCRATES

Your enemy will pay you back with rage, will make you suffer, but the biggest damage to you will be caused by the rage and hatred existing in your heart. Neither your father, nor your mother, nor all your family can make you more good than your heart can when it forgives and forgets its abuse.
—DHAMMAPADA, a book of BUDDHIST WISDOM

Your rage cannot be justified by anything. The reason for your rage is always inside you.

January 24

Nobody knows where the human race is going. The highest wisdom, then, is to know where *you* should go: toward perfection.

A wise man seeks wisdom; a madman thinks that he has found it.

—PERSIAN PROVERB

It is not the place we occupy which is important, but the direction in which we move.

—OLIVER WENDELL HOLMES

Your actions should be determined not by the desire of the people around you, but by the needs of all mankind.

There is a basic knowledge which is necessary for every human being; until a person has acquired this basic knowledge, all other kinds of knowledge will be harmful for him.

Socrates told his students that in good systems of education, there is a certain limit you should not go beyond. In geometry, he said, it is enough to know how to measure the land when you want to sell it or buy it, or how to share an inheritance, or to divide work among workers. He did not like too many sophisticated sciences; though he knew all of them. He said that sophisticated knowledge requires an extra effort that takes the student's time from the most basic and the most important human pursuit: moral perfection.

—XENOPHON

Divert your gaze from the world of lies. Do not trust your feelings. Only in yourself, only in your impersonal self, can you find the eternal.

—DHAMMAPADA, a book of BUDDHIST WISDOM

It is better to know several basic rules of life than to study many unnecessary sciences. The major rules of life will stop you from evil and show you the good path in life; but the knowledge of many unnecessary sciences may lead you into the temptation of pride, and stop you from understanding the basic rules of life.

A rich man cannot be merciful. If he becomes really merciful, he will quickly lose his riches.

Stop robbing others before you give money to beggars. With the same hand that we rob one person, we reward another, giving to the poor the money which we have taken from the even poorer. Better no charity than this kind of charity.

—SAINT JOHN CHRYSOSTOM

The best example of the cruelty of the rich man's life is his effort to become virtuous.

But whoso hath this world's good, and seeth his brother have need, and shutteth up his bowels of compassion from him, how dwelleth the love of God in him?
   My little children, let us not love in word; neither in tongue; but in deed and truth.

—I JOHN 3:17–18

In order to love not with word and tongue, but in deed and truth, everyone should help those who ask for help, so Christ said.
   But if you start giving to all those who ask, even if you are very rich, very soon you will not be rich anymore.

Love for other people gives a real feeling of good, and it unites you with other people and with God.

A wise man loves not because he wants to profit from it but because he finds bliss in love itself.

Do not regret the past. What is the use of regrets? The lie says that you should regret. The truth says you should be filled with love. Push all sad memories away from you. Do not speak of the past. Live in the light of love, and all things will be given to you.

—PERSIAN WISDOM

They asked a Chinese man, "What is science?" He said, "Science is knowing people." Then they asked, "And what is virtue?" He answered, "Virtue is loving people."

Just as a mother puts her life at risk to guard and save her only child, so every person should guard and save in himself love for every living being.

The fearlessness, calm, inner peace, and joy which are given to us by love are so big that all other things in the world cannot be compared with them, especially for the person who understands the real blessing of love.

For a person to know the law that makes him free, he must be elevated from a material to a spiritual life.

I have many things to say and to judge on you: but he that sent me is true; and I speak to the world those things which I have heard of him. They understood not that he spake to them of the Father. Then said Jesus unto them, When ye have lifted up the Son of man, then shall ye know that I am he, and that I do nothing of myself; but as my Father hath taught me, I speak these things.

—JOHN 8:26–28

"I and God are the same," said the teacher. If you think that my spiritual being is God, you are mistaken. But my real self is close to God, and to other people. In order to understand this part of myself, you should elevate the man inside of you. When you elevate the man inside of you, then you will see that there is no difference between him and any other person on earth.

It only seems as if we differ from each other. A flower on a blossoming tree can think that it is a separate being, but all flowers are parts of the same blossoming of one apple tree, and they all come from one seed.

We live a short period of time in this world, but we live it according to the laws of eternal life.
—After HENRY DAVID THOREAU

Submission to the law created by men makes one a slave; obedience to the law created by God makes one free.

Wisdom is knowing the purpose of life, and knowing how to achieve it.

You can achieve wisdom in three ways. The first way is the way of meditation. This is the most noble way. The second way is the way of imitation. This is the easiest and least satisfying way. Thirdly, there is the way of experience. This is the most difficult way.

—CONFUCIUS

The merit of a man is not in the knowledge he possesses, but in the effort he made to achieve it.

—GOTTHOLD EPHRAIM LESSING

If you want to study yourself—look into the hearts of other people. If you want to study other people—look into your own heart.

—FRIEDRICH VON SCHILLER

Your soul is both your judge and your place of sanctuary. Your own soul is your highest judge.

—MANU

There is nothing in which real wisdom cannot be displayed.

When Socrates was asked where he came from, he said that he was a citizen of the world. He regarded himself as a citizen of the universe.

—MARCUS TULLIUS CICERO

When people wanted to kill a bear in the ancient times, they hung a heavy log over a bowl of honey. The bear would push the log away in order to eat the honey. The log would swing back and hit the bear. The bear would become irritated and push the log even harder, and it would return and hit him harder in return. This would continue until the log killed the bear. People behave in the same way when they return evil for the evil they receive from other people. Can't people be wiser than bears?

You should respond with kindness toward evil done to you, and you will destroy in an evil person that pleasure which he derives from evil.

The true teaching of love is strong; it kills evil before evil can grow and become powerful.

Only greatly insolent people establish a religious law which is to be taken for granted by others, which should be accepted by everyone on faith, without any discussion or doubts.

Why must people do this?

What a strange thing! Many scoundrels try to disguise their dirty deeds by their dedication to the interests of religion, or by their high morals, or by love for their motherland.

—HEINRICH HEINE

But be not yet called Rabbi: for one is your Master, even Christ; and all ye are brethren. And call no man your father upon the earth: for one is your Father, which is in heaven. Neither be ye called masters: for one is your Master, even Christ.

—MATTHEW 23:8–10

The essence of the teaching of Christ is to follow his commandments. Those who just repeat, "My God, My Lord" will not get to heaven; only those who fulfill God's will.

February 1

It is not possible to explain the origin of the spiritual from the material.

A man consists of body and soul. Thus often, especially in his youth, he is interested only in his body, but nevertheless, the most essential part of every man is not his body, but his soul. It is your soul that you must take care of, not your body. You must learn this over time, and remember that your real life is in your spirit, that is, in your soul. Save it from everyday dirt and do not let your flesh guide it; subdue your body to your soul, and then you will fulfill your destiny and live a happy life.

—After MARCUS AURELIUS

The heart of the matter is whether we believe or disbelieve in the existence of a spiritual realm. All people are divided into two groups, those who are alive and those who are dead; in other words, those who believe and those who don't.

An unbeliever says: "What is spirit! . . . What I ate and what I enjoyed, this is what I possess, this is material and real!" And such a person, without thinking much, takes care only of the outer things, arranging in order only his own mean, dirty affairs; he becomes a liar, a snob, a slave, and does not feel any higher needs: freedom, truth, and love. Such a person keeps away from the light of the intellect, because in fact he is dead, and this light gives life only to living things, and hardens and rots the dead things.

—ALEXANDR ARKHANGELSKY

The difference between the spiritual realm and the material is equally clear and obvious, both for a child and a wise man; further speculations are not necessary.

February 2

There are two different states of human existence: first, to live without thinking of death; second, to live with the thought that you approach death with every hour of your life.

The more you transform your life from the material to the spiritual domain, the less you become afraid of death. A person who lives a truly spiritual life has no fear of death.

When you have doubts about what to do, just imagine that you might die at the end of that same day, and then all your doubts will disappear, and you will see clearly what your conscience tells you, and what is your true personal wish.

A man condemned to immediate execution will not think about the growth of his estate, or about achieving glory, or about the victory of one group over another, or about the discovery of a new planet. But one minute before his death a man may wish to console an abused person, or help an old person to stand up, or to put a bandage on someone's injury, or to repair a toy for a child.

February 3

Kindness is for your soul as health is for your body: you do not notice it when you have it.

A person becomes happy to the same extent to which he or she gives happiness to other people.

—JEREMY BENTHAM

The will of God for us is to live in happiness and to take an interest in the lives of others.

—JOHN RUSKIN

Love is real only when a person can sacrifice himself for another person. Only when a person forgets himself for the sake of another, and lives for another creature, only this kind of love can be called true love, and only in this love do we see the blessing and reward of life. This is the foundation of the world.

Nothing can make our life, or the lives of other people, more beautiful than perpetual kindness.

February 4

A man is free only when he lives in truth, and the truth may be perceived only by the intellect.

If you throw some nuts and cookies on a road, you will eventually see children come, pick them up, and start to argue and fight for them. Adults would not fight for such things. And even children would not pick up the nuts' empty shells.

For a wise man, the wealth, the glory, and the rewards of this world are like sweets or empty shells on a road. Let the children pick them up and fight for them. Let them kiss the hands of the rich men, the rulers, and their servants. For the wise one, all these are but empty shells.

—EPICTETUS

A distinctive feature of a thinking person is submission to his fate, as opposed to the shameful struggle with it that is a characteristic feature of animals.

—MARCUS AURELIUS

We are not free in this world, subdued by our passions and by the emotions of other people to the degree that we forget the requirements of our intellects. If we really want to become free, we can be so only through our intellect.

February 5

All events, whether in the lives of human individuals, or human societies, have their beginnings in thought. Therefore, to fully understand other people and other societies, we must look beyond previous events to the thoughts which gave rise to them.

Perhaps it is even more important to know what one should not think about than what one should think about.

Our thoughts, depending on whether they are good or bad, can bring us either to paradise or to hell; this happens, neither in heaven nor under the earth, but here, in this life.

—LUCY MALORY

A thought seems to be free and independent, but a human being has something stronger than thought, something which could guide our thoughts.

In order to change the nature of things, either within yourself or in others, one should change, not the events, but those thoughts which created those events.

February 6

Sexual desire is the most all-consuming of desires. This desire is never sated, for the more it is satisfied, the more it grows.

Very often people are made proud by their control over their own desires, and by the force and passion with which they master them. What a strange delusion!

Many people worry, and suffer, because they have been involved in so many bad things in their lives. In truth, though, good things often happen in spite of our wishes, and sometimes even in opposition to our wishes, and often after our excitement and suffering over unworthy things.

Remember how passionately you yearned in the past for many of the things which you hate or despise now.

Remember how many things you lost trying to satisfy your former desires. The same thing could happen now, with the desires which excite you at present. Try to tame your present desires, calm them; this is most beneficial, and most achievable.

February 7

Perfecting the self is both an inner and an outer work: You cannot improve yourself without communicating with other people, influencing them, and being influenced by them.

Three temptations torture people: sexual desire, pride, and lust for wealth. All the misfortunes of mankind come from these three cravings. Without them, people would live in happiness. But how can we get rid of these terrible illnesses? . . . Work on yourself and improve yourself; this is the answer. Start the improvement of this world from within.

—F. Robert de Lamennais

"Be perfect, as your heavenly Father," Christ said. This does not mean that Christ asked people to be as good as God; only that everyone should strive for perfection.

Pure perfection can be found only in God; one's life consists of becoming closer to God. And when a person knows that good is good and that evil is evil, then he or she gets closer to good, and moves farther from evil.

—Confucius

There is nothing more harmful to you than improving only your material, animal side of life. There is nothing more beneficial, both for you and for others, than activity directed to the improvement of your soul.

February 8

Why do people like to blame others so much? He who casts blame on another person is quick to think that he would not do the very same thing. It is the same with people who like to listen to the fault-finding of their neighbors.

When two people have a dispute, both are to blame. And therefore, a dispute will stop only when at least one person understands that he or she is guilty.

Judge not, that ye be not judged. For with what judgment ye judge, ye shall be judged: and with what measure ye mete, it shall be measured to you again.

—MATTHEW 7:1–2

Stop blaming other people, and you will feel what an alcoholic feels when he stops drinking, or what a smoker feels when he stops smoking. You will feel that you have brought relief to your soul.

The material evil caused by war is big, but it is incomparably small in comparison with the perversion or the understanding of good and bad which happens during the war, and which is put into the souls of people who do not think.

A child meets another child with a smile, displaying his friendly attitude and joy. This same behavior lives in all sincere people. But very often, a man from one nation already hates a man from another nation, and is ready to cause him sufferings and even death, even before he meets him. Those who create these feelings in nations commit a terrible crime!

The most powerful weapon known is the weapon of blessing. Therefore, a clever person relies on it. He wins with peace, not with war.

—LAO-TZU

War creates a state in which power and glory is at the end too often received by the most undeserving and vicious people.

February 10

The higher the opinion a person has of himself, the more unstable is his position; the lower he moves in his self-esteem, the firmer he stands.

To be strong, you have to be like water: if there are no obstacles, it flows; if there is an obstacle it stops; if a dam is broken, then it flows further; if a vessel is square, then it has a square form; if a vessel is round, then it has a round form. Because it is so soft and flexible, it is the most necessary and the strongest thing.

—LAO-TZU

The more a person analyzes his inner self, the more insignificant he seems to himself. This is the first lesson of wisdom. Let us be humble, and we will become wise. Let us know our weakness, and it will give us power.

—WILLIAM ELLERY CHANNING

Water does not stay on a mountaintop, but flows into the valley. In the same manner, real virtue does not remain with those people who want to be higher than the others; but virtue stays only with people who are humble.

—After the TALMUD

Try to find out your potential. After you know it, do not be afraid to underestimate it. Be cautious not to exaggerate it.

February 11

A person's life is good only to the extent that it fulfills the expectations of the will of God.

Evil, in the form of suffering and death, is everywhere apparent to a person who accepts the law of his material, animal existence as the major law of his life. Only when a man lowers himself to the state of an animal does death and suffering scare him. The only road open for him to escape that fear is the road of fulfillment of the law of God, the law which is expressed in love. There is no death and no suffering for a man who lives according to the law of God.

Be as you are, as you have to be, and the rest is God's business.

—HENRI AMIEL

The fulfillment of our duties and the satisfaction of our personal pleasures are two different things. Duties have their own laws, and even if we try to mix our duties with our pleasures, they will separate themselves.

—After IMMANUEL KANT

We know the law of God, both as it is presented to us by the different religions of the world and as our own conscience, when it is not obscured by passion and prejudice, and we can easily understand the applications of this law to our life, for all real good stems from its requirements.

February 12

It is obvious for everyone that death expects us all in the long run; but nevertheless we live our lives as if there will be no death.

If only God is among us, and eternity exists, then everything is different. We can distinguish good from evil, light from darkness, and despair disappears.

—ERASMUS

One of the key questions we face is whether our lives end after death. Whether we believe in eternity or not determines our actions. Therefore, it is crucial that we determine what is mortal in us, and what is eternal, and that we cherish those things eternal. Most people do exactly the opposite.

—After BLAISE PASCAL

The more deeply you understand life, the less you grieve over the destruction caused by death.

Whatever name you give to the origin of man, this spiritual quality of humans to understand, feel, and exist, it is holy, it is divine, and, therefore, it should be eternal.

—MARCUS TULLIUS CICERO

February 13

Religion is a philosophy which can be understood by anyone.

A person can please God only with the godliness of his life. If an outwardly faithful person is not good, clear, and humble in his life, then he presents a big lie, he serves God falsely.
—After IMMANUEL KANT

Religion is simple wisdom which is directed to the heart and understood by the intellect.

Religion can enlighten philosophical meditations; philosophical meditations can strengthen religion. Therefore, try to communicate both with truly religious people and truly good philosophers, alive and dead.

February 14

A holy spirit lives within you.

Jesus answered and said unto him, Verily, verily, I say unto thee, Except a man be born again, he cannot see the kingdom of God.

—JOHN 3:3

Intellect can be enlightened only in a kind person. A person can be kind only when he has an enlightened intellect. One helps the other.

—CHINESE WISDOM

A merchant married a princess, and he built a palace for her, bought luxurious dresses for her, and brought her hundreds of servants to make her happy. But the princess was bored. She was missing something, and she constantly thought about her royal origin. Thus it is with a human soul: you can surround it with all the pleasures on earth, but it will still be missing its home, the beginning which is called God, the place from which it has originated.

—After the TALMUD

Even if people do not know what real kindness is, they nevertheless have it within them.

—CONFUCIUS

God lives in every one of us. When a person remembers this, the thought of it can save him from evil, and help him to do good.

February 15

There is simplicity of nature, and there is simplicity of wisdom. Both of them evoke love and respect.

The greatest truth is the most simple one.

When people speak in a very elaborate and sophisticated way, they either want to tell a lie, or to admire themselves. You should not believe such people. Good speech is always clear, clever, and understood by all.

Simplicity is the consequence of refined emotions.
—JEAN D'ALEMBERT

Words can unite people. Therefore, try to speak very clearly, and tell only the truth, for nothing can unite people more than truth and simplicity.

February 16

The younger and the more primitive a person is, the more he or she believes that life is material and that it exists only in the body. The older and wiser a person becomes, the more he or she understands that all life originates from the spirit.

Look at the sky, and at the earth, and think that all things pass. All of the mountains and rivers you see, and all the forms of life, and all creations of nature, all pass. Then you will understand the truth; you will see what remains, what does not pass.

—BUDDHIST WISDOM

Remember that you are not mortal; only your body is mortal. What is alive is not your body but the spirit living in your body. An unseen force guides your body, just as an unseen force guides the world.

—After MARCUS TULLIUS CICERO

A person can understand his real destination in life only after he manages to liberate himself from the sensual, material world.

February 17

All people of the world have an equal right to the privileges of this world.

Equality cannot be reached, as some people think, only by civil measures. It can be reached only by love of God and people, and this love can be reached, not by civil measures, but only as the result of spiritual learning.

They say that equality is not possible, because some people will always be stronger or smarter than others. But it is exactly because of this, said Lichtenberg, precisely because some people are stronger and smarter than others, that the principle of equality is necessary. The advantages of the rich over the poor demonstrate not only inequality of force and intellect, but inequality of civil rights.

Christ revealed to humanity those things which their best selves already knew: that people are equal because the same spirit lives in all of them. . . . Learn from the small children, behave like children, and treat all people on an equal basis, with love and tenderness.

February 18

Personality is a mask which disguises the divine being which lives in every person. The more one rejects personality, the more this divine beginning is manifested.

You must love only God, and you must hate only yourself.

—BLAISE PASCAL

Therefore doth my Father love me, because I lay down my life, that I might take it again. No man taketh it from me, but I lay it down of myself. I have power to lay it down, and I have power to take it again. This commandment have I received of my Father.

—JOHN 10:17–18

Only those people who deny their own personality can understand the religious teaching.

—The TALMUD

He who wants to save his soul, will lose it; and he who wants to lose his life for me and the new testament, will save it.

—MARK 8:35

Those who do not see the meaning of their life in temporary things, in their names and bodies, those people know the truth of life.

—DHAMMAPADA, a book of BUDDHIST WISDOM

Only when we forget about ourselves, when we get out of the thoughts of ourselves, can we fruitfully communicate with others, listen to them, and influence them.

February 19

It is a sin not to be engaged in work, even if it is not necessary for you to make your living with everyday work.

One of the best and purest joys is having a rest after labor.
—IMMANUEL KANT

Work all the time. Do not think that work is a disaster for you, and do not seek praise or reward for your work.
—MARCUS AURELIUS

The most outstanding gifts can be destroyed by idleness.
—MICHEL DE MONTAIGNE

Nothing can make a person feel more noble than work. Without work, a person cannot have human dignity. It is because of this that idle people are so much concerned by the superficial, outer expression of their importance; they know that without this, other people would despise them.

When we accept truth and repent our sins, we understand that nobody can have special rights, advantages, or privileges in this life. There is no end or limit to our duties and obligations. And the first and the most important obligation for us is to fight with nature for our life and for the lives of other people.

Humankind goes on without stopping. This movement forward is necessary for you as an individual as well. If you want to serve God, you should be a worker for the spiritual progress of humanity.

The way of life of any people depends on their faith. Faith, with time, becomes more simple, more clear, and closer to the real truth, and in accordance with the simplifying and clarifying of faith, people become more and more united.

If you think it is ever warranted to stop on the path of further understanding, you are very far from the truth. The life which we received was given to us not that we might just admire it, but that we should ever look for new truth hidden from us.

—After JOHN MILTON

Mankind makes progress when its faith progresses. And if there is any progress in religion, it is not in the discovery of something new, but in the purifying of the truths which have been revealed and explained to us.

We should not substitute real religious progress with other types of progress: technical, scholarly, and artistic. These technical, scholarly, and artistic achievements can certainly coexist with religious backwardness, as happens in our time.

If you want to serve God, you should work on the side of religious progress in the fight against prejudice, toward a better understanding of the clear and pure religion.

February 21

There was a time when people ate each other. They no longer do so, but they still eat animals. The time will come when more and more people will drop this terrible habit.

It is a mistake to believe that we need obey no moral in our attitude to the animals, that we have no moral responsibilities to them. This way lies complete vulgarity and rudeness.
—ARTHUR SCHOPENHAUER

The killing and eating of animals is a prejudice accepted by those who think that animals were given to people by God to eat, so that there is nothing wrong in killing them. This is not true. It may be written in some books that it is not a sin to kill an animal, but it is written in our own hearts more clearly than in any books—that we should take pity on animals in the same way as we do on each other. And we all know this, if we do not deaden the voice of our conscience inside of us.

February 22

All that is written about God, and all that people say about Him, still falls short of the mark. Certain things, which every person can *understand* about God, can never be expressed, things necessary for everyone, and things which cause the love of God.

—After Angelus Silesius

An intellect which can be understood is not an eternal intellect; a being which can be named is not an eternal being.

—Lao-Tzu

There is a force which resides in all things, without which there is no heaven and no earth. This force cannot be perceived. People try to describe its qualities, to give it different names, such as "intellect" or "love," but the being itself has no name. It is very remote from us, and it is closest to us.

—After Lao-Tzu

God is the limitless being which accepts only truth.

—Matthew Arnold

Those people who ask where God is are crazy; God is everywhere, in all of nature and in the soul of each person. There are many different religions, but there is only one God. If a person cannot understand himself, how can he understand God?

—Indian wisdom

If your eyes become blinded by the sun, you do not say that the sun does not exist. In the same way, you should not say that God does not exist if your intellect is lost in trying to understand him.

—After Angelus Silesius

February 23

The existing design of life corresponds neither to the requirements of conscience nor to the requirements of intellect.

Imagine a flock of pigeons in a corn field. Imagine that ninety-nine of them, instead of pecking the corn they need and using it as they need it, start to collect all they can into one big heap. Imagine that they do not leave much corn for themselves, but save this big heap of corn on behalf of the vilest and worst in their flock. Imagine that they all sit in a circle and watch this one pigeon, who squanders and wastes this wealth. And then imagine that they rush at a weak pigeon who is the most hungry among them who darest to take one grain from the heap without permission, and they punish him.

If you can imagine this, then you can understand the day-to-day behavior of mankind.

—WILLIAM PALEY

I see people arguing with each other, preparing different traps for each other, lying and betraying each other. I cannot see without tears that the foundations of Good and Evil are forgotten, or in some cases completely unknown.

—THEOGNIS

People are rational creatures. Why do they seem capable of using violence so much more easily than reason in their interactions with each other?

February 24

For a truth to be heard, it must be spoken with kindness. Truth is kind only when it is spoken through your heart with sincerity. You should know that when a message you convey to another person is not understood by him, at least one of the following things is true: what you have said is not true, or you have conveyed it without kindness.

The only way to tell the truth is to speak with kindness. Only the words of a loving man can be heard.

—HENRY DAVID THOREAU

To tell the truth is the same as to be a good tailor, or to be a good farmer, or to write beautifully. To be good at any activity requires practice: no matter how hard you try, you cannot do naturally what you have not done repeatedly. In order to get accustomed to speaking the truth, you should tell only the truth, even in the smallest of things.

We lie to other people so often that we get used to it, and we start to lie to ourselves.

—FRANÇOIS DE LA ROCHEFOUCAULD

Truth cannot make a person unkind, or too self-assured; the manifestations of truth telling are humility and simplicity.

To pray is to accept and to remember the laws of the limitless being, God, and to measure all your deeds—past, present, and future—according to His laws.

Before you start praying, ask yourself whether at that moment you can concentrate; otherwise, do not pray at all.

Those who make a habit out of prayer do not pray sincerely.

—The TALMUD

If you ask for support from God, then you will learn how to find it in yourself. He does not change us, but we change ourselves by getting closer to Him. All ask from Him, as if He should help us, but in the end we give these things to ourselves.

—JEAN JACQUES ROUSSEAU

From the ancient times, it has been known that prayer is a human necessity.

People use different rituals during prayer, special addresses in special circumstances, in special places, in the ways they present their message to God and ask Him to be kind.

But let there be this constant: during a prayer, forget about all external worldly things and address the divine part of your soul. Use this divine part to gain communication with that of which it is a part and when you feel yourself close to God, you deliver your soul to Him, and show Him all your deeds and wishes. Prayer does not happen according to the requirements of the world, but according to the divine part of your soul.

February 26

After a long conversation, stop and try to remember what you have just discussed. Don't be surprised if many things, sometimes even everything you have discussed, were meaningless, empty, and trivial, and sometimes even bad.

A stupid person should keep silent. But if he knew this, he would not be a stupid person.

—Muslih-ud-Din Saadi

Only speak when your words are better than your silence.

—Arabic proverb

For every time you regret that you did not say something, you will regret a hundred times that you did not keep your silence.

Kind people are never involved in arguments, and those who like to argue are never kind. Truthful words are not always pleasant, and pleasant words are not necessarily truthful.

—Lao-Tzu

If you want to be a clever person, you have to learn how to ask cleverly, how to listen attentively, how to respond quietly, and how to stop talking when there is nothing more to say.

Many stupid things are uttered by people whose only motivation is to say something original.

—Voltaire

If you have time to think before you start talking, think, Is it necessary to speak? Will what I have to say harm anyone?

February 27

A charity is only then a real charity when it involves sacrifice.

Your gold and silver is cankered; and the rust of them shall be a witness against you, and shall eat your flesh as it were fire.

—JAMES 5:3

In money—in the money itself, in its acquisition, in its possession—there is something immoral.

A truly kind person cannot be rich. A rich person, without question, is not a kind one.

—CHINESE PROVERB

Then said Jesus unto his disciples, Verily I say unto you, that a rich man shall hardly enter into the kingdom of heaven. And again I say unto you, it is easier for a camel to go through the eye of a needle, than for a rich man to enter into the kingdom of God.

—MATTHEW 19:23–24

February 28

Art is one of the means of unifying people.

If beautiful art does not express moral ideas, ideas which unite people, then it is not art, but only entertainment. People need to be entertained in order to distance themselves from disappointment in their lives.

—IMMANUEL KANT

It is possible to imagine that art could die, but it is not possible to imagine that real art could live if it became a slave of wealth that laughed at the poor.

Art is one of the most powerful means of convincing people of anything, both good and bad; therefore, you must be very careful in its use.

An artist is one of two things: he is either a high priest, or a more or less smart entertainer.

—GIUSEPPE MAZZINI

Meditations or discussions about art are the most useless pastimes known. Those who really know art know that art can speak well with its own language, and that to speak about art with words is useless. Most people who speak about art do not understand or feel real art.

To move, you must know where to go, in terms both of everyday motion and of your whole life. In order to live a good life, you must know where life leads.

Perfection is of God. To wish for perfection is of man.
—JOHANN WOLFGANG VON GOETHE

Life is not given to us that we might live idly without work. No, our life is a struggle and a journey. Good should struggle with evil; truth should struggle with falsehood; freedom should struggle with slavery; love should struggle with hatred. Life is movement, a walk along the way of life to the fulfillment of those ideas which illuminate us, both in our intellect and in our hearts, with divine light.
—After GIUSEPPE MAZZINI

The ideal is within you, and the obstacle to reaching this ideal is also within you. You already possess all the material from which to create your ideal self.
—THOMAS CARLYLE

We should believe that the goodness which exists in us and in this world will be fulfilled. This is the major condition to make it happen.

March 1

The fear of death in man is the understanding of his sins.

The more spiritual a life a person leads, the less he is afraid of death. For a spiritual person death means setting the spirit free from the body. Such a person knows that the things with which he lives cannot be destroyed.

Only those who do not live are not afraid of death.

If, as Socrates said, death is the state in which we abide during our sleep made permanent, we all know this state, and know there is nothing terrible in it. And if death is a transfer to a better life, as many people think, then death is not evil but a blessing.

We should get ready for death, because it will come, sooner or later. The best thing to do is to live a good life. If you live a good life, you should not be afraid of death.

March 2

The more closely a person unites with the will of God, the firmer this person becomes in his actions.

When a traveler starts on a trip along a road which is under the threat of robbers, he does not go alone. He waits for a friend, someone to be his escort, and then he follows him and so is protected from robbers. A wise man lives his life the same way. But there are so many troubles in this world. How can we stand all of them? What kind of a friend or escort will we find on our way, so that we may pass through our lives without fear? Where should we turn? There is only one answer, only one real friend. That is God.

If you follow God everywhere, you will steer clear of trouble. To follow God is to want what He wants, and not to want what He does not want. How to achieve this? You have to understand and follow His laws.

—After EPICTETUS

Do not wish for too much, nor think that the things you wish for are the only right or necessary things. You should wish only for those things for which God wishes.

—HENRI AMIEL

The right path in life is very narrow, but it is important to find it. You can understand it, as well as we can understand it, as a walkway of wood built across a swamp; if you step off it, you will plunge into the swamp of misunderstanding and evil. A wise man returns to the true path at once, but a weak man plunges further and further into the swamp, and it becomes more and more difficult for him to get out.

March 3

What reward should a good deed bring you? Only the joy you receive by performing it. And any other reward lessens the feeling of this joy.

He who does good to others makes the biggest gift to himself.

—LUCIUS ANNAEUS SENECA

A saint prayed to God in the following way: "O God, please be kind to evil people as much as you are to kind people. Kind people already feel good, because they are kind."

—MUSLIH-UD-DIN SAADI

If you do good and ask for a reward, you weaken the force of your goodness.

—From the BOOK OF DIVINE THOUGHTS

Do not let your left hand know what your right hand is doing.

—MATTHEW 6:3

What a joy it is to do a good deed! And this joy is strongest if no one knows that you have done it.

March 4

Eating to excess is a vice just as bad as many others. We often do not notice it in others, because most of us are subject to it.

There are sins against others, and sins against yourself. You commit sins against others when you do not respect God's spirit in them; you commit sins against yourself when you do not respect God's spirit in yourself. One of the most common sins against yourself is gluttony.

A person who overeats cannot fight laziness; and a lazy man cannot fight sexual dissipation. All spiritual teachings start with restrictions, with control of the appetite.

God gave food to people, and the devil gave cooks.

Socrates, a wise man, tried to abstain from all unnecessary things. He said that food should serve you in fighting your hunger, and not in developing sophisticated tastes, and he asked his students to follow his rule. He reminded his students about the wise Odysseus, whom Circe, an evil sorceress, could not subject to her magic, because he did not eat to excess. But the members of his crew, his friends, were turned into a herd of pigs by her as soon as they rushed to the abundance of sweet food.

Look at your mouth; through it, when you eat to excess, illnesses enter your body. Behave in such a way that when you finish your dinner, you want to eat a little more.

Eating to excess is not considered to be a sin by many, because it produces no noticeable harm. But there are sins which destroy human dignity, and eating to excess is one such sin.

March 5

Just as it's folly to try to lift yourself into the air, you should not praise yourself too much. When you praise yourself, you produce the opposite effect in others, and appear lower in their eyes.

If you want other people to speak well of you, do not speak well of yourself.

—Blaise Pascal

A man who praises himself does not see anything except himself around him. It is better to be a blind man than to see only yourself and nobody else.

—Muslih-ud-Din Saadi

He who always listens to what other people say about him will never find inner peace.

A flatterer speaks his flattery because he has a low opinion of himself and of others.

—Jean de La Bruyère

If you want to preserve your good name, do not praise yourself and do not so much as allow others to praise you.

March 6

Love of God is love in itself; it is love for the sake of love. This kind of love is the highest blessing. It does not allow the slightest possibility of treating even a single creature without love; if there is even one person whom you do not love, then you lose God's love and blessing.

Love of your neighbor without love of God is a plant without roots. You should love God—this love is a real and firm love. It does not become weaker, only stronger, and it gives good to those who have it.

Some say that you should be afraid of God. Not true; you have to love God. How can you love those whom you are afraid of? God is love, and how can you be afraid of love? No, you should not fear God, but love Him. And if you love God, then you will not be afraid of Him, or anything else in the world.

March 7

Physical work, physical exercise for your body, is a necessary condition of life. A man can force others to do things for him, but he cannot free himself from the necessity of his own physical work. And if a man does not work at necessary and good things, then he will work at unnecessary and stupid things.

Work, the process of work in itself, is the most important thing for us, and its reward should be of minor importance; if it is, you please your creator, God. If the reward is of major importance for you, and the work itself of minor importance, then you are the slave of the reward and its creator, the devil, and even the lowest and the least among all devils.

—JOHN RUSKIN

A European praised the advantages of mechanized labor to a Chinese man: "This invention relieves a man from the need for physical work." But the Chinese man replied, "Physical work is good. Being relieved from physical work will be an enormous disaster."

Every physical labor makes a man more noble. If you do not teach your son some physical skills, you teach him to rob others.

—After the TALMUD

Without exercise of their muscles, neither man nor animal can live.

So that this exercise may give you joy and satisfaction, do good physical work. This is also the best way to serve others.

March 8

Prayer is a time to remind yourself of your attitude to limitless things, to God.

Through prayer, you establish your attitude to the beginning of everything; you clarify your attitude toward people, your relationship with and your duties to them, and to the Father of all of us.

—After the TALMUD

It is good to pray at the same time each day. If you cannot collect your thoughts, better not to pray, because you should always pray with your heart, not simply repeat words with your tongue.

It is good and necessary to pray in solitude, but is also good to pray when you are in the crowd, when you are excited or irritated—to think about your soul and about God.

Do not think that you can please God with prayer. You will please God by submitting to Him. Prayer is just a reminder for you of who you are and what the purpose of your life is.

March 9

War and Christianity are not compatible.

War is one of the worst, most terrible things in this world.

War in this world can be stopped not by the ruling establishment, but by those who suffer from the war. They will do the most natural thing: stop obeying orders.

The armed world and the wars it wages will be destroyed one day, but not by the kings or the rulers of this world. War is profitable for them. War will stop the moment the people who suffer from war fully understand that it is evil.

March 10

That which gives life is the same in all things.

All living creatures fear pain and death. Try to understand yourself in every living creature: do not torture and do not kill. Stop suffering and death. All living creatures want what you want; all living creatures praise their lives.
—DHAMMAPADA, a book of BUDDHIST WISDOM

All living creatures have the same divine beginning, all are in unity. We are all members of one great body.

Nature created us related to each other, from the same material, for the same purpose. Because of this, somewhere within all of us is mutual love for each other.
—LUCIUS ANNAEUS SENECA

There is only one right pathway of life. Sooner or later, we all will meet each other on this pathway. The understanding of it is very clearly inscribed in our hearts, and it is wide and easy to find. At the end of this way is God, and He calls us to Himself. It is so painful to watch people who miss this way of life and go along the other pathway, the way of death.

—After NIKOLAI GOGOL

Expunge from yourself anything which interferes with your feeling of a special connection between yourself and all living creatures.

March 11

Food is necessary for the life of an individual, and marriage is necessary for the life of humanity. If eating to excess is evil for an individual, then excess in marriage and sexuality creates evil both for individuals and for human society.

A marriage is a special obligation between two people, of opposite sexes, to have children only with each other. To break this pact is a lie, a deception, and a crime.

It is a great thing when two souls are united to support each other in their work, in their successes and misfortunes, until the last silent minutes of the last good-bye.

—GEORGE ELIOT

The Pharisees also came unto him, tempting him, and saying unto him, Is it lawful for a man to put away his wife for every cause? And he answered and said unto them, Have ye not read, that he which made them at the beginning made them male and female, and said, For this cause shall a man leave father and mother, and shall cleave to his wife: and they twain shall be one flesh? Wherefore they are no more twain, but one flesh. What therefore God hath joined together, let not man put asunder.

—MATTHEW 19:3–6

The unification of a man and a woman for the continuation of humankind is a great and important deed for every individual, as well as for all mankind. You cannot do it as it pleases you, or as you like it. You have to do it in the way which was thought and set out by the wise and holy people who have lived before us.

March 12

The deeds of a person become his life, become his fate. This is the law of our life.

The Persians have such a fable: After death, a soul flew into the sky, and met a terrible woman, a dirty and horrible apparition, with festered sores discharging pus, who was going in the opposite direction. "What are you doing here?" asked the soul. "Who are you?" The terrible woman answered, "I am your deeds."

It is important not only to talk about the good life but to do good things.

—After the TALMUD

Never postpone a good deed which you can do now, because death does not choose whether you have or haven't done the things you should have done. Death waits for nobody and nothing. It has neither enemies, nor friends.

—INDIAN WISDOM

When you appeared in this world, you cried, and all the people around you rejoiced. You have to live your life in such a way that when you leave this world, you will rejoice, and all the people around you will cry.

—INDIAN WISDOM

Your past deeds weigh heavily on the future direction of your life; but sometimes, you can change this direction through the effort of your spirit.

March 13

The condition of wisdom is purity; the consequence of wisdom is the peace of your soul.

A man who follows his wishes changes his attitude with time. Very soon he is not satisfied any more with the things he does.

Those people who have nothing to lose are very rich.

—CHINESE PROVERB

A wise person never considers himself to be wise. And a person never considers himself wise when he has the image of God before him.

Wisdom is limitless, and the closer you approach it, the more important it becomes for your life.
   A person can always improve himself.

March 14

Love brings people to unification. The universal intellect, which is the same for everyone, supports this unification.

Look around. What do the world's people think about it? They think about everything except what is most important. They think about dancing, music, and singing; they think about houses, wealth, and power; they are jealous about the wealth of rich people and kings; but they do not think at all about what it means to be human.

— After BLAISE PASCAL

One of the major responsibilities of a person is to make that intellectual spark which you have received from heaven illuminate the world around you.

— CHINESE WISDOM

Everything in this world is the manifestation of the divine intellect.

All that we know, we know through the intellect. Those who do not believe, people who say that you should not follow your intellect, remind me of those who suggest that you turn down the only lantern which shows you the way into the darkness.

March 15

Be filled with love for other people, including those who are unpleasant or hostile to you. A real trial to one's love is to love your enemies.

If you love your enemies, you will have no enemies.

The most perfect among men is he who loves his neighbor without thinking about whether the person is good or bad.

—MOHAMMED

Be humble and oppose dissipation. Even a thin sword cannot cut soft silk. Using tender words and kindness, you can lead an elephant with a hair.

—MUSLIH-UD-DIN SAADI

Every time you are abused by someone and feel animosity toward him, remember that all people are children of God. Regardless of whether this person is unpleasant to you, you should not stop loving him as your brother, because, as much as you are, he is God's son.

March 16

Modern science cannot study *everything*; without being supported by religion, science does not know what it should study.

Real wisdom is not the knowledge of everything, but the knowledge of which things in life are necessary, which are less necessary, and which are completely unnecessary to know. Among the most necessary knowledge is the knowledge of how to live well, that is, how to produce the least possible evil and the greatest goodness in one's life. At present, people study useless sciences, but forget to study this, the most important knowledge.

A person who knows little likes to talk, and one who knows much mostly keeps silent.

This is because a person who knows little thinks that everything he knows is important, and wants to tell everyone. A person who knows much also knows that there is much more he doesn't know. That's why he speaks only when it is necessary to speak, and when he is not asked questions, he keeps his silence.

—After Jean Jacques Rousseau

If all knowledge were good, then pursuit of every sort of knowledge would be useful. But many false meditations are disguised as good and useful knowledge; therefore, be strict in selecting the knowledge you want to acquire.

March 17

We can improve this world only by distributing the true faith among the world's people.

A society cannot live without a united faith and purpose. All social activity cannot really improve our social life if it is not based on the foundations established by religion.

—GIUSEPPE MAZZINI

The apostles lived united, in such a way that they shared one heart and soul. If they had not, no one today would know about Christianity. When some pagans did not accept Christianity, it was because they did not see complete unification and love among Christians. We Christians are to blame when other people do not accept the Christian faith.

—After SAINT JOHN CHRYSOSTOM

Christianity in its pure and sincere form works like dynamite: it blows up old mountains and opens up new, limitless horizons.

If you see that some aspect of your society is bad, and you want to improve it, there is only one way to do so: you have to improve people. And in order to improve people, you begin with only one thing: you can become better yourself.

March 18

Blaming other people is always wrong, because no one knows what has happened and happens in the soul of another person.

We often make judgments about other people. We call one person kind, the other stupid, the third evil, the fourth clever. But we should not do so. A man changes constantly; he flows like a river, and every new day he differs from what he was before. He was stupid and became clever; he was evil and became kind at heart; and so on. You cannot judge another person. The moment you blame him, he becomes someone different.

If you want to correct your failings, you do not have the time to waste in blaming other people.

Never blame your neighbor until you have been in his place.
—The TALMUD

Forgive other people for many things, but do not forgive yourself anything.

—PUBLILIUS SYRUS

I know of myself that I do not wish to do evil. If I do evil, it is because I cannot restrain myself. It is the same with other people: they usually do evil because they cannot restrain themselves from evil. Therefore, why do I think badly of other people? Why should I blame them?

March 19

The creation of the world would have been a very bad act were it right for rich people to live off the work of the poor, and yet think that they were the benefactors.

A stone falls on a pot—woe to the pot; a pot falls on a stone—woe to the pot; in every case, it is bad for the pot.
—The TALMUD

The pleasures of the rich are often acquired by the tears of the poor.

Wealth is created by the concentration of human labor; usually one people produce labor, and others concentrate it. This is called "the division of labor" by contemporary wise people.

There is something wrong with the creation of this world, because the rich people think that they are the benefactors of the poor, but in fact those rich are fed and dressed by the work of these poor and live in luxury created for them by the poor.

Those who live according to the will of God cannot be sensitive to the judgments of other people.

You should think in such a way that everybody could look into your soul and see what is transpiring there.

—LUCIUS ANNAEUS SENECA

Live in the open.

—AUGUSTE COMTE

It is not good to hide your bad deeds, but it is even worse to flaunt them in the open and to be proud of them.

To feel shame in the company of other people is good, but it is even better to experience shame when you are alone with yourself.

Do not hide anything from other people when they ask you, but do not boast about bad things if you are not asked about them.

You can hide some things from other people, but you cannot hide anything from God.

For nothing is secret, that shall not be made manifest; neither any thing hid, that shall not be known and come to light.

—LUKE 8:17

Live your life in such a way that you neither hide nor have a wish to display your life to people.

March 21

We know our life as it exists only here, in this world; therefore, if our life is to have any meaning, it should be here in this world.

Do not wish for death just because your life is hard. All the burdens on your shoulders will help you fulfill your destiny. The only way to get rid of your burdens is to live your life in such a way that you fulfill your destiny.

—RALPH WALDO EMERSON

Real life is found only in the present. If people tell you that you should live your life preparing for the future, do not believe them. We live in this life, and we know this life only, and therefore all our efforts should be directed toward the improvement of this life. Not your life in general but every hour of this life should be lived in the best way you know how.

Life is neither suffering nor pleasure, but the business which we have to do, and which we have to finish honestly, up to our life's end.

—ALEXIS DE TOCQUEVILLE

This world, only this world, is the place of our work, and all our forces, all our efforts, should be directed toward this life.

March 22

If truth makes our life easier, then it is better to accept the truth than to hide from it. Our life can be changed, but the truth cannot be changed: it will always remain the truth, and it will expose us.

We should live our lives as if everyone could see us, as if the most secret corners of our soul were open to the sight of others. Why should we hide anything? You cannot hide anything from God. All divine and human learning can be summarized in one truth—that we are members of one big body. Nature united us in one big family, and we should live our lives together, helping each other.

—After Lucius Annaeus Seneca

Seek the truth: it always shows us what we should do, what we should not do, and what we should stop doing.

March 23

The earth, the air, and the sun belong to all of us; they cannot be made objects of property.

We are all visitors in this world. Wherever you go in this world, to the north, to the south, to the west, or to the east, there will always be a man waiting to tell you, "This is my property. Get out of here!" When you visit other countries in the world and you come back, you will see that there is not a single piece of free land where your wife can give birth to your child, where you can stop and start working on the land, and where your children can find rest for your bones at life's end.

—After F. ROBERT DE LAMENNAIS

If you leave a man on land which is someone else's property and tell him that he is a completely free man and can work for himself, it's as if you drop him in the middle of the Atlantic and tell him that he is free to go ashore.

—HENRY GEORGE

Those who own land in amounts larger than that which is needed to feed their own families can be treated as being guilty of causing the poverty of many other people.

March 24

Only the person who fulfills God's law can understand God. The more closely he fulfills God's law, the better he understands God.

There is not a single believer who from time to time has not had some hesitations about the existence of God. But these moments of hesitation are not harmful. On the contrary, they lead us to a better understanding of God.

Seeking God with your soul is a process that has limitless sides and aspects.

Moses said to God, "Where can I find you?" God said, "If you are looking for me, you have already found me."

They asked a wise man, "How do you know that God exists?" He replied, "Is it necessary to have a torch in order to see the sun?" We do not have enough words to explain what God is, but we know without words that He exists.

—ARABIC WISDOM

Jews consider it a sin to state the name of God aloud. They are right: God is spirit, and every name is material and not spiritual.

March 25

During our lives we help each other: sometimes we help other people, sometimes we are helped by others. But the world is formed so that usually some people mostly help others, and some mostly receive their help.

As you acquire objects, and you use them, you should keep in mind that they are the products of people's work. When you damage or destroy these objects, you damage or destroy the toil, and this part of the life, of other people.

Look at all of your knowledge as a gift, as a means of helping other people.

A strong and wise person uses his gifts to support other people.

—JOHN RUSKIN

Help should be mutual. Moreover, those who accept help and assistance from their brothers should pay them back, not only with money, but with love, respect, and gratitude.

March 26

The most important change that can occur in a person's life is a change in his faith.

Individuals die, but the wisdom they have obtained in their lives does not die with them. Mankind keeps all this wisdom, and a person uses the wisdom of those who lived before him. The education of mankind reminds me of the creation of the ancient pyramids, in that everyone who lives puts another stone in the foundation.

We are temporary visitors in this world; after we are educated, we are called to different places, and we pass away. But the general education of mankind goes on, very slowly but without interruption.

—After GIUSEPPE MAZZINI

It is a big mistake to think that faith is immutable, that it does not change over generations. The longer mankind exists, its faith becomes simpler and stronger. And the simpler and stronger our faith becomes, the better we live.

If you believe that faith is the same for all times and that it cannot be changed, you might just as well believe that those fairy tales and proverbs and children's stories which your grandmother told you when you were a small baby are real, and that you ought to believe in them all your life.

March 27

The more a person believes in God, the less he is afraid of other people.

Do not despair. Do not be disappointed if you see that you cannot accomplish all the good which you would like to accomplish. If you fall, try to stand up; try to overcome the obstacle before you. Get to the heart of the matter, to the essence of things.

—MARCUS AURELIUS

Those who fear people do not fear God; those who fear God do not fear people.

He who is not afraid of anything, and who is ready to give his life for a righteous cause, is much stronger than he whom other people fear and who has the lives of other people in his power.

Look for the better men among those who are despised.

Do what you think is necessary, and do not expect reward. Remember that a stupid person is a bad judge of clever deeds.

You want to save yourself from the power of other people—give yourself to the power of God. If you see yourself as being in the power of God, then people cannot do anything to you.

March 28

Wisdom can be achieved by inner work, through solitary communication with yourself; it also can be achieved when you communicate with other people.

Listen and be attentive, but do not speak too much; and when you are asked a question, answer briefly. Do not be ashamed to accept that sometimes you do not know an answer to what you were asked. Do not get into an argument just for the sake of argument; and do not boast.

—SUFI WISDOM

You can view your own drawbacks only through the eyes of other people.

—CHINESE PROVERB

I have learned many things from my teachers; I have learned many things from my friends; and I have learned even more from my students.

—The TALMUD

If you see a holy man, think: how could I become like him? If you see a dissipated man, think: don't I have the same vices?

—CHINESE WISDOM

Real love is not in words but in deeds, and only love can give you real wisdom.

When you are in company, do not forget what you have found out when you were thinking in solitude; and when you are meditating in solitude, think about what you found out by communicating with other people.

March 29

If sometimes you feel that in spite of all your wishes to gain triumph over your passions, they gain victory over you, do not think that you cannot conquer them at all. You have only proven that you weren't able to this one time. A good groom does not drop his reins when he cannot stop his horses at once but tries again to pull the reins, and eventually the horses stop. So if you could not resist the temptations once, continue your fight, and in the end not your passion but you will gain the victory.

Try to be the master over greed, sloth, lechery, and rage.

A victory over oneself is a bigger and a better victory than a victory over thousands of people in a score of battles. Those who have achieved victory over other people can be defeated in future battles, but those who have achieved victory over themselves become victors forever.
—DHAMMAPADA, a book of BUDDHIST WISDOM

A passion in a person's heart is like a spider's web. At the beginning it is an alien visitor; then it becomes a regular guest; then it becomes master of the house.
—After the TALMUD

He who has achieved victory over himself has real power.
—EASTERN WISDOM

Abstention cannot be achieved at once, but it should be a process, and a constant effort. The life of a person who makes this effort is directed not to the calming of his passions but to the mastery of them.

Time and persistence help you in these efforts.

March 30

The truth is not only a joy, it is an instrument in conflict much more powerful than violence.

Then came Peter to him, and said, Lord, how oft shall my brother sin against me, and I forgive him? till seven times?

Jesus saith unto him, I say not unto thee, Until seven times: but, Until seventy times seven.

—Matthew 18:21–22

If you want to demonstrate some truth to your listeners, do not be irritated, and do not say unkind or abusive words.

—After Epictetus

If you notice someone in error, then correct this person and his mistake in a humble way. If he does not listen to you, blame yourself only; or, even better, do not blame anybody, but continue to be humble.

—Marcus Aurelius

If you have parted from a person, and he was not satisfied with you, or did not agree with you when you were right, he is not to blame, but probably it is you who are to blame, because you were not kind enough with this man.

March 31

To repent means to show your vices and weaknesses to all. Repentance means taking responsibility for all of the bad things you have done, purifying your soul, and preparing to accept goodness.

When a kind man does not accept his mistakes and tries always to justify himself, he becomes an unkind man.

Do you have qualities which can be criticized and improved? Try to admit that this is so, and to find these qualities out by yourself.

Nothing can make a person's soul softer than the understanding of his own blame, and nothing can make one harder than the desire always to be right.

—After the TALMUD

Those who cover their old sins with present-day good deeds remind me of the moonlight which illuminates this dark world on a cloudy night.

— DHAMMAPADA, a book of BUDDHIST WISDOM

A man will always understand his sins as well as his limits in this limitless world.

April 1

Science can be divided into an infinite number of disciplines, and the amount of knowledge that can be pursued in each discipline is limitless. The most critical piece of knowledge, then, is the knowledge of what is essential to learn and what isn't.

A huge amount of knowledge is accumulated at present. Soon our abilities will be too weak, and our lives too short, to study this knowledge. We have vast treasures of knowledge at our disposal but after we study them, we often do not use them at all. It would be better not to have this burden, this unnecessary knowledge, which we do not really need.

—IMMANUEL KANT

Too-voracious reading, begun at too early an age, fills our minds with undigested material. Our memory can become the master of our feelings and our fate; and when it does, an intellectual effort is required to reinforce our feelings with primeval innocence, to find ourselves amidst the dusty heaps of foreign thoughts and viewpoints, in order to start feeling by ourselves, and—I am ready to say—in order to live on our own.

—GEORGE LICHTENBERG

Beware of false knowledge. All evil comes from it.

Knowledge is limitless. Therefore, there is a minuscule difference between those who know a lot and those who know very little.

April 2

The only real life is one lived close to God. This does not happen by itself; you must make an effort to make this happen, and this effort will bring you joy.

A habit is never good, even a habit of doing good deeds. Good deeds, after they become habits, are no longer acts of virtue. Real good is achieved only with effort.

—IMMANUEL KANT

When you carry your burden, you should know that it is good for you to have it. Make the best of this burden and take from it everything which is necessary for your intellectual life, as your stomach takes from food everything necessary for your flesh, or as fire burns brighter after you put some wood on it.

—MARCUS AURELIUS

Be attentive to what you do; never consider anything unworthy of your attention.

—CONFUCIUS

Spiritual effort and the joy that comes from understanding life go hand in hand like physical exertion and rest. Without physical exertion, there is no joy in rest; without spiritual effort, there can be no joyful understanding of life.

April 3

When I die, only one of two things can happen: either this essence which I understand as myself will transform into a different being, or I will stop being a separate individual and become a part of God. Either possibility is good.

Death is the destruction of this body with which I understand the world in this life. It is the destruction of the glass through which I look at the world. And we do not know whether this glass will be replaced by another; or whether the essence which looks through the window will integrate with the world. We cannot know this.

There is a certain limit to the appropriate length of any time in this world. Just as the fruits and vegetables are limited by the seasons of the year, everything should have its beginning, its life, and its ending, after which it should pass away. Wise people willingly submit to this order.

—MARCUS TULLIUS CICERO

All that I know about God brings me to the following conclusion: all that He did for us were the best things possible.

—After RALPH WALDO EMERSON

You should live your life so that you are not afraid of death, and at the same time do not wish to die.

April 4

Life should and can be limitless joy.

Life in this world is not a vale of tears, not a trial, but a thing that surpasses our imagination. Life could be limitless joy, if we would only take it for what it is, in the way it is given to us.

A person's unfriendly attitude to other people makes life unhappy, both for that person and for those who surround him. A friendly mood and loving attitude are as an oil which lubricates the wheels of life, making them move easily and smoothly.

Try to live your life and be happy with your destiny, acquiring inner peace by love and good deeds.
                                                    —Marcus Aurelius

The secret of happiness? Enjoy small pleasures.
                                                    —Samuel Smiles

Do not seek pleasure everywhere, but always be ready to find it.

                                                    —John Ruskin

A truly wise man is always joyful.

The best way to live joyfully is to believe that life was given for joy. When joy disappears, look for your mistake.

April 5

It is difficult to avoid working in life without either sinning, committing violence, being a party to violence, or by flattering and pleasing the agents of violence.

Being poor is better than living in luxury and serving the rich. Do not stand at the door of a rich man asking for favors if you hope to lead a good life.

—INDIAN PROVERB

A dress presented to you as a gift by the king may be beautiful, but your own simple dress is better. Different meals from the tables of the rich may be good, but a loaf of simple bread from your own table always tastes much better.

—MUSLIH-UD-DIN SAADI

To those people who do not work the land, the soil says: if you do not work me, by applying physical labor with both of your hands, then you will stand in front of the doors of others asking for help; you will always be fated to use the leftovers of the rich.

—ZOROASTER

You will find that people unwilling to work will either take advantage of others or be humiliated by them.

April 6

People involve themselves in countless activities which they consider to be important, but they forget about one activity which is more important and necessary than any other, and which includes all other things: the improvement of their soul.

The biggest happiness is when at the end of the year you feel better than at the beginning.
—HENRY DAVID THOREAU

"Be perfect, as your Father in heaven is perfect." This means that you should try to find the presence of the Holy Spirit in your soul.

To improve ourselves, to move toward that goal, perfection, that puts no less a demand on us for being unattainable, requires solitude, removal from the concerns of everyday life. And yet constant solitude renders self-improvement impossible, if not pointless. A balance must be struck between meditating in solitude and then applying this to your everyday life.

April 7

To repay evil with goodness is easier, wiser, and more natural than to repay evil with evil.

Repay evil with goodness.

—The TALMUD

And when they were come to the place, which is called Calvary, there they crucified him, and the malefactors, one on the right hand, and the other on the left. Then said Jesus, Father, forgive them; for they know not what they do.

—LUKE 23:33–34

Conquer rage with humility, conquer evil with goodness, conquer greed with generosity, and conquer lies with truth.
—DHAMMAPADA, a book of BUDDHIST WISDOM

When we treat our neighbors as they deserve to be treated, we make them even worse; when we treat them as if they were who we wish they were, we improve them.
—JOHANN WOLFGANG VON GOETHE

Those who take joy in repaying an evil with goodness will always try to experience this joy again.

April 8

People think that if they call mass murder "war," then mass murder will stop being a murder, a crime.

One can deny Christ in various ways: one can blaspheme rudely, or mock his greatness. But such ways are not dangerous; religion is too precious for people, and this mockery cannot cleave them from it. But there is another way to deny Christ: this is when you call Him your master, and you claim to follow His commandments, but you suppress any free thought by quoting his words, and disguise all stupidities, all mistakes, and all sins of the people in his name. This second way is the truly dangerous one.

—THEODORE PARKER

It is not true that a war against a foreign nation can be sacred. It is not true that the earth wants blood. The earth wants pure water from the sky for its rivers, pure dew from its clouds, but not blood. War is cursed by God, as are those who participate in it.

—ALFRED DE VIGNY

And because lawlessness is increased, most people's love will grow cold.

Rather, it is your crimes that separate you from God, and it is your sins that make him hide his face so that he will not hear you. For your hands are stained with blood, your fingers with guilt; your lips speak falsehood, and your tongue utters deceit.

—ISAIAH 59:2–3

Murder is always a crime, no matter whom, and how it is justified.

April 9

Love of goodness and faith in immortality are inseparable.

Nobody can say that he knows what the afterlife will be. Our beliefs are based not on logical proofs but on moral ones and therefore I cannot say that God exists and I am immortal, but I can say that God exists and that my "self" is immortal. This means that my faith in God is so closely connected with my nature that this faith cannot be separated from me.

—Immanuel Kant

The animal beginning disappears, the veil is taken from the future, the darkness disperses. It is then that we feel our immortality.

—After Saint Martin

We live in this world like a child who enters a room where a clever person is speaking. The child did not hear the beginning of the speech, and he leaves before the end; and there are certain things which he hears but does not understand. In the same way, the great speech of God started many, many centuries before we started learning, and it will continue for many centuries after we turn to dust. We hear only part of it, and we do not understand the biggest part of what we hear, but nevertheless, a bit vaguely, we understand something great, something important.

If you truly love goodness (God), then you cannot have doubts in your immortality.

April 10

The holy spirit which exists in people is liberated more and more. This will change our existing world order.

Real science shows us how to apply our religious faith to our outer lives. Art shows us how to apply it to our feelings.

The further any purpose the faster we should work toward it.
—GIUSEPPE MAZZINI

The longer I live, the more things I must complete.
—WILLIAM ELLERY CHANNING

The more we understand our divine nature, the more its rules should be fulfilled in our actions.

Everything is connected more closely in the spiritual world than in the material world. Every lie brings multiple lies, every cruelty brings more cruelty.

Very often people are proud of the purity of their conscience only because their memory is too short.

—ZANIZAD RAFAEZSKY

Drop after drop, water fills the vessel; in the same way those who want to be good, become filled with goodness.

—DHAMMAPADA, a book of BUDDHIST WISDOM

Many of our vices exist only because they are supported by other vices; therefore, if we destroy our major vices, many others will disappear at once, in the same way as branches fall when you cut the trunk of a tree.

—BLAISE PASCAL

Be attentive to the appearance of evil. There is an inner voice in your soul which always tells you about approaching evil. You feel unpleasant, you feel ashamed. Believe in this voice; stop and seek to improve yourself, and then you will defeat evil.

April 12

At a certain level of self-awareness, a person understands something supernatural in himself.

God exists because we exist. You can call it any other name, but there is no doubt that the superior life which created us exists. And you can call the source of this life God, or give it any other name.

—GIUSEPPE MAZZINI

God exists only for those who look for Him. Start looking: you will find Him in you and yourself in Him.

Looking for God is like pulling a net in the water. When you pull the net, it is heavy and full of water, and yet when you pull it out, there is nothing in it. When you seek God with your intellect and your actions, God exists in you, and as soon as you decide that you have found God, and stop and become satisfied, you have lost him.

—FYODOR STRAKHOV

It is surprising that I could not see a very simple truth: behind and above this world and our lives, there is someone who knows why this world exists and why we exist in this world. And our lives are as bubbles in boiling water, which appear, rise to the surface, pop, and disappear.

The unity of all living beings exists in this world where everybody and everything quietly seeks God. It is only unbelieving atheists who see eternal silence.

—JEAN JACQUES ROUSSEAU

Just because a person does not understand God, he has no right to draw the conclusion that God does not exist.

April 13

We understand the divine, spiritual beginning of our life both with our intellect and with our love.

A man is wise who does three things: first, he does by himself those things which he advises others to do; secondly, he does not do anything that contravenes the truth; and thirdly, he is patient with the weaknesses of those who surround him.

Great thoughts come directly from the heart.
—Luc de Vauvenargues

Investigate everything: believe only in those things which exist in accordance with intellect.

A clever person cannot be evil. A kind person is always clever. Improve your kindness by exercising your intellect, and improve your intellect by exercising your kindness and love.

April 14

We cannot hope to obtain any sort of perfection in a society which is divided into two parts: rich people who rule the world and poor people who obey their orders.

We came to strange conclusions in this world: we say that we live in society but at the same time we live lonely lives.

—THOMAS CARLYLE

If there are millionaires, there should be paupers.

—HENRY GEORGE

If you have an income without working hard, then someone worked hard without receiving an income.

—MAIMONIDES

It is worse to be an oppressive master than an obedient slave. Excessive wealth is worse than poverty.

April 15

The consequences of our notions cannot be known to us, because they ripple outward limitlessly in a limitless world.

Our efforts to penetrate the mystery of God are futile. It is enough to follow the divine law.

—The TALMUD

A saint lives with his inner life; he denies outer life.

—LAO-TZU

Our most important actions are those consequences which we will not see.

Great deeds have very remote consequences.

—JOHN RUSKIN

If you can see all of the consequences of your actions, then your actions are of no use.

April 16

To accept the dignity of another person is an axiom. It has nothing to do with subduing, supporting, or giving charity to other people.

The smallest detail can benefit the strengthening of character. Do not say that small details are not important; only a person with high morals can see their importance.

Some of the most religious people in Russia have an interesting habit: they make a low bow to persons to whom they are introduced for the first time. They say they do this to acknowledge the divine spirit that every person has within himself. This is not a widespread tradition, but its foundations are very deep.

A man is humble. He can hardly say: I exist, I can think.
—After RALPH WALDO EMERSON

A person should know that he performs true charity not in front of other persons, but before the eternal law of God.

April 17

Christianity is the study of the divine beginning in a person.

Christianity is a very simple thing: love other persons, as you love God. Be as perfect as your father in heaven. Live in the spirit of God, making the best things, in the best possible way, for the best purposes. Even a small child can understand these ideas, and even a great mind cannot improve upon them.

—THEODORE PARKER

Without the clear understanding of the meaning of one's life, without faith, a person can at any minute deny good and start worshiping evil.

A person cannot have complete understanding of the meaning of life. A person can only know its direction.

The essence of all religious teachings is love. What is special in Christianity is teachings about love, the clear and exact statement of the major condition of love: nonresistance to evil and violence.

If you want to be quiet and strong, work and improve your faith.

April 18

What is important is not the quantity of your knowledge, but its quality. You can know many things without knowing that which is most important.

Ignorance in itself is neither shameful nor harmful. Nobody can know everything. But pretending that you know what you actually do not know is both shameful and harmful.

There are two types of ignorance, the pure, natural ignorance into which all people are born, and the ignorance of the so-called wise. You will see that many among those who call themselves scholars do not know real life, and they despise simple people and simple things.

—BLAISE PASCAL

The truth should often overcome thousands of obstacles, until it is accepted.

—GEORGE LICHTENBERG

The scholar who thinks but does not create is like the cloud which does not give rain.

—EASTERN WISDOM

Vague and complex terminology was created by false scholars. Real, truthful knowledge does not need vague terms.

April 19

A man who does not understand the benefit of suffering does not live a clever and true life.

Mankind has never achieved greatness but through suffering.

—F. ROBERT DE LAMENNAIS

Without suffering, spiritual growth cannot happen. Suffering often accompanies death, but suffering is also a useful, beneficial condition of life. It is said that God loves those who experience suffering.

Religion gives a person the understanding of the meaning of his existence and his destination.

—ANATOLE FRANCE

A person who lives a spiritual life cannot help but see that suffering brings him closer to God. Seen in this light, suffering loses its bitter side and becomes bliss.

April 20

For a person who leads a spiritual life, self-sacrifice brings a bliss that far transcends the pleasure of a person who lives by the self-indulgent satisfaction of his animal passions.

He who is kind does good for other people. And if a person suffers while he does kind deeds, he becomes an even better person.

—JEAN DE LA BRUYÈRE

He that loveth father or mother more than me is not worthy of me: and he that loveth son or daughter more than me is not worthy of me.

—MATTHEW 10:37

There is no higher blessing for a person than to do charitable work for the benefit and well-being of others.

—LUCY MALORY

Just as fire blows out candles, good deeds for the benefit of others destroy a selfish life.

The dark spot in the sunlight that falls on us is the shadow created by our own personalities. We live for ourselves only when we live for others. It may seem strange, but try it, and you will see it from your own experience.

April 21

In the future, the order of the social life of the Christian world will be changed by the replacement of violence and its fears with love and blessing.

Thus I command you, to love one another.

—JOHN 15:17–19

It is a mistake to think that there are times when you can safely address a person without love. You can work with objects without love—cutting wood, baking bricks, making iron—but you cannot work with people without love. In the same way as you cannot work with bees without being cautious, you cannot work with people without being mindful of their humanity. It is the quality of people as it is of bees: if you are not very cautious with them, then you harm both yourself and them. It cannot be otherwise, because mutual love is the major law of our existence.

Until I can see that the major commandment of Christ—love your enemies—is being fulfilled, I will continue to believe that many people are not real Christians, but only pretend to be Christians.

—GOTTHOLD EPHRAIM LESSING

The worst mistake which was ever made in this world was the separation of political science from ethics.

—PERCY BYSSHE SHELLEY

You should live so that it is possible to create the kingdom of love on earth. You should live a life based not on violence but on love.

*The greatest knowledge is self-knowledge. He who under-
stands himself will understand God.*

Jesus cried and said, He that believeth on me, believeth
not on me, but on him that sent me. And he that seeth me
seeth him that sent me. I am come a light into the world,
that whosoever believeth on me should not abide in darkness. And if any man hear my words, and believe not, I
judge him not: for I came not to judge the world, but to
save the world. He that rejecteth me, and receiveth not
my words, hath one that judgeth him: the word that I
have spoken, the same shall judge him in the last day. For
I have not spoken of myself; but the Father which sent
me, he gave me a commandment, what I should say, and
what I should speak. And I know that this commandment
is life everlasting: whatsoever I speak therefore, even as
the Father said unto me, so I speak.

—JOHN 12:44–50

Without purity of soul, how can you say, I will glorify
God? That light, like a morning star, which lives in the
heart of every person, this light is our salvation.

—WABANA PURANA, INDIAN WISDOM

A person can transform his personality, his inner self, from
the domain of suffering and subduing into the domain
which is always steady and joyful, that is, the domain of
understanding his spiritual and divine essence.

April 23

Real goodness is always simple.

Simplicity is so attractive and so profitable that it is strange that so few people lead truly simple lives.

Do not seek happiness elsewhere. Give thanks to God, who made necessary things simple, and complicated things unnecessary.

—GREGORY SKOVORODA

Most of our spending is done to forward our efforts to look like others.

—RALPH WALDO EMERSON

Every great thing is done in a quiet, humble, simple way; to plow the land, to build houses, to breed cattle, even to think—you cannot do such things when there are thunder and lightning around you. Great and true things are always simple and humble.

No one looks less simple than those people who artificially strive to seem so. Artificial simplicity is the most unpleasant of all artificial things.

In any struggle true bravery lies within those who know that God is their ally.

Whatever happens, do not lose faith. Nothing bad can happen to you as a human being.

These things I have spoken unto you, that in me ye might have peace. In the world ye shall have tribulation: but be of good cheer; I have overcome the world.

—JOHN 16:33

Everything is indefinite, misty, and transient; only virtue is clear, and it cannot be destroyed by any force.

—MARCUS TULLIUS CICERO

Only a person who renounces his personality becomes truly powerful. As soon as one denies his personality, it is not he but God who acts through him.

Once upon a time, a Roman empress lost her precious jewelry. It was announced across the empire that whoever found her lost stones before thirty days would receive a big reward, but any who returned the jewelry after thirty days would be executed. Samuel, a Jewish rabbi, found the precious stones, but he returned them after thirty days had passed. "Have you been abroad?" the Roman empress asked him. "No, I was at home." "Maybe you did not know what was proclaimed?" "No, I knew," said Samuel. "Then why did you not return these things before the expiry of the thirty days? Now you have to be executed." "I wanted to show you that I returned your lost jewelry, not because of fear of your punishment, but because of fear of God."

April 25

A person can understand himself as a material or a spiritual being. When you understand yourself as a spiritual being, then you are free.

What is "love of God," if it is not the effort to add part of yourself to the higher creative flow of energy in this world? Divine force exists in everything, but the greatest manifestation of it in this world is in humanity, and in order to put it to work, one must understand it and accept it.

If a person does not believe himself capable of doing the best things in the world, then he starts to create the worst things.

I know that the sky knows everything, and that its laws are constant. I know that it sees everything, it gets into everything, and it is present in everything. The heavens can get into the depths of all human hearts in the same way that the daylight can lighten a dark room. We should try to reflect this heavenly light.

—CHINESE WISDOM

April 26

The understanding of the existence of God is accessible to everybody; the complete understanding of the essence of God is not accessible to any person.

All the nations of the world name and respect God. Different people give him different names, and put different clothes on him; but there is only one God under all these different manifestations.

—JEAN JACQUES ROUSSEAU

Faith in God is as natural to men as their ability to walk on two feet. This faith can be modified, and it can even disappear in some individuals; but as a rule, it is necessary for intellectual life in society.

—After GEORGE LICHTENBERG

There are some statements which cannot be fathomed: God exists or he does not exist; the soul exists in the body, or we do not have a soul; the world was created or the world was not created.

—BLAISE PASCAL

Live in God, live together with God, by understanding Him in you, and do not try to define Him with words.

April 27

A bad mood is often the reason for blaming others; but very often blaming others causes bad feelings in us: the more we blame others, the worse we feel.

One of our most common and widespread prejudices is that every person has a fixed, special characteristic, that there are kind people and evil, clever people and stupid people, and cold or hot people. But people are not like this; we can say about a person only that he is more often kind than evil, more often clever than stupid, more often cold than hot. We always divide people like this, but it is no less wrong.

If there is animosity between two people, both are to blame. Any number you multiply by zero, however big, will equal zero. If there is animosity, then, it is the animosity of two people toward each other, and it exists in both of them.

Try to understand and remember that a person always tries to do what is best for himself. And if he is right when he does the best thing for himself, it is good; but if he is mistaken, it is bad, because suffering will follow after such mistakes.

If you remember this, then you will never be upset by anybody, you will never reproach anybody, and you will never be an enemy to anybody.

—After EPICTETUS

If you are living with another person, make an agreement that as soon as either of you starts to blame the other, you will end the argument.

April 28

Work is the necessary condition of happiness. First, favorite and free work; secondly, the physical work which arouses your appetite and afterward gives you tranquil and sound sleep.

Manual labor does not exclude intellectual activity, but improves its quality and even helps it.

Constant idleness should be included in the tortures of hell, but it is, on the contrary, considered to be one of the joys of paradise.

—CHARLES DE MONTESQUIEU

When a person sets to work, even if it is the most unqualified, primitive, simple work, the human soul calms down. As soon as a person starts to work, all the demons leave him and cannot approach him. A man becomes a man.

—THOMAS CARLYLE

Work is necessary. If you want a good disposition of your spirit, work until you become tired. But not too much. Not until you become exhausted. A good spiritual disposition can be destroyed by excessive work as well as by idleness.

A person can fulfill his purpose in life equally as well in illness as in health.

If we meditate upon the existence of life after death, then all illnesses would seem to be taking us closer to the movement from one life to another, a transfer more desirable than undesirable. During these pains we can understand and explain for ourselves what will happen to us, and prepare for the new state of our next existence.

Usually people think that it is possible to serve God and humanity only when you are healthy. This is not true. Very often it is to the contrary. Christ served God and all mankind when he suffered on the cross, and even then he forgave those who killed him. Every person can do likewise. You cannot say which state is better, a healthy or ill state, in the service of God and humankind.

For yourself, and for yourself only, it is necessary to have health and power. But to serve God it is not necessary, and sometimes even the opposite is true.

Very often, when I have dealt with terminally ill people, I have learned that the most important thing is not hiding the approaching death from the patient, but on the contrary, explaining to him his own divine, spiritual nature, which grows in him and which cannot be destroyed by death.

Illnesses almost always destroy one's physical power, and they release the power of one's soul. For a person who concentrates his consciousness in the spiritual domain, illnesses do not diminish his goodness, but on the contrary, they increase it.

April 30

It seems that it is impossible to live without discovering the purpose of your life. And the first thing which a person should do is to understand the meaning of life. But the majority of people who consider themselves to be educated are proud that they have reached such a great height that they cease to care about the meaning of existence.

The real purpose of our existence is to understand this limitless life existing in this world.

A person may not know the purpose of his life, but he should know *how* to live.

A worker at a big plant may not necessarily know the purpose of his labor, but if he is a good worker, he should know how to do well what he should do.

Every living being has sensory organs which reveal to it its place in the world. For a human, the primary sense is the intellect.

If you do not know your place in the world and the meaning of your life, you should know that there is something to blame; and it is not the social system, or your intellect, but the way in which you directed your intellect.

May 1

He who sees his life as a process of spiritual perfection does not fear external events.

Abu Ganifakh died in a prison in Baghdad in which he'd been put by Caliph al-Mansur for refusing to accept the teaching of Kaad. Once, before his death, when this famous spiritual teacher received a heavy blow from a guard, he told the man who hit him, "I could render you an injury after you have done an injury to me. I could complain to the Caliph, but I will not complain. In my prayers, I could tell God about this offense which you have done to me, but I will refrain from this. During the day of the Final Judgment I could ask divine revenge for your act, but even if this day comes today, and even if I knew that my prayer would be heard, even then I would enter paradise only with you."

—PERSIAN WISDOM

Do not think that courage lies only in boldness and power. The highest courage is the courage to be higher than your rage and to love a person who has offended you.

—PERSIAN WISDOM

Criticize yourself, but do not feel desperate about it.

—EPICTETUS

What I tell you in darkness, that speak ye in light: and what ye hear in the ear, that preach ye upon the house-tops. And fear not them which kill the body, but are not able to kill the soul: but rather fear him which is able to destroy both soul and body in hell.

—MATTHEW 10:27–28

May 2

People very often do not accept the truth, because they do not like the form in which the truth is presented to them.

The beginning of a quarrel is like a flood which breaks through a dam. As soon as it rushes through, you cannot stop it.

—The TALMUD

One should avoid disputes; when a fire becomes too big, it is difficult to quell it.

During an argument, make your words very soft, and your heart hard. Do not try to lash out at your opponent, but try to convince him.

—GEORGE WILKINS

If you know the truth, or if you think that you know the truth, try to pass it on to the others, as simply as you can, along with the feeling of love for those persons to whom you pass it.

May 3

The life of Jesus Christ is very important for us as an example of a life of one who could not see the fruits of his work during his lifetime.

Clever people study in order to know more. Undeserving people study to be more known.

—EASTERN WISDOM

In order to reach spiritual perfection, you should first of all take care of the purity of your soul. This can be reached when the heart looks for truth, and strives for wholeness, and depends on true knowledge.

—CONFUCIUS

If you would like to know how to recognize a prophet, look to him who gives you the knowledge of your own heart.

—PERSIAN WISDOM

Every person has only one purpose: to find perfection in goodness. Therefore, only that knowledge is necessary which leads us to this.

May 4

Every thought which is expressed by words is a force, and this force is limitless.

Good thoughts which originate from the hearts of men are as useful as good examples.

—LUCIUS ANNAEUS SENECA

Strong thoughts which are expressed in a powerful way aid the improvement of life.

—MARCUS TULLIUS CICERO

A thought is an intellectual and vital energy of life, and it can be either a curse or a blessing, depending on its quality.

—LUCY MALORY

Truth expressed in words is the greatest force there is in the lives of people. We do not understand this force completely, because its consequences are never seen at once.

Use good thoughts of wise people; if you cannot create similar kind and wise thoughts, then at least do not distribute the false thoughts expressed by you and by others.

May 5

Religious teaching, that is, the explanation of the purpose and meaning of life, should be the basis of any education.

People think that it is no crime to lie to children, and that to lie to children is not really very wrong, but even sometimes necessary. But it is clear that with children you should be especially careful and honest about what you say to them.

You should always be truthful, especially with a child. You should always do what you have promised him, otherwise you will teach him to lie.

—After the TALMUD

Man, whose teacher is nature, should not be a piece of wax on which an elevated image of some professor is to be carved.

—GEORGE LICHTENBERG

Do not say to a child whom you teach that there is a final truth, if you do not believe in something completely, or if you have some doubts. To do such a thing is a great crime.

May 6

Compassion for animals is so natural to us that we can become insensitive to their suffering and death only through traditions or hypnosis.

Compassion for animals is so closely connected with kindness that you can truly say that a person cannot be kind if he is cruel to animals. Compassion for animals comes from the same source as compassion toward people.

—ARTHUR SCHOPENHAUER

Fear God, do not torture animals. Let them serve you, and let them rest when they are tired; provide enough food and drink for those creatures which cannot speak.

—MOHAMMED

A person is not higher than other animals because he can mercilessly torture them, but because he can take pity on them.

—BUDDHIST WISDOM

Do not allow your children to kill insects; this is the first step along a road which can lead to the killing of people.

—PYTHAGORAS

May 7

A person who tries to find good outside himself, either in this life or in the one to come, is making a mistake.

I went along all the earth, searching for a guiding light. I went all over without rest, at night and during the day, and then I heard from a preacher, who opened the truth to me, that the answer is inside my soul, and that the light which I was looking for everywhere in the world is inside me.

—EASTERN WISDOM

There are no coincidences, either in life or in one's fate. A man creates his own destiny.

—ABEL VILLEMAIN

You either make evil for yourself, or you escape sin and purify yourself; you are bad or evil, or you are pure; and nobody can save you except for yourself.

—DHAMMAPADA, a book of BUDDHIST WISDOM

Your body is a city which is full of good and evil; and you are the king of this city and your intellect is your best counselor.

—SAINT LUKE

The happiness or unhappiness of a man does not depend upon the amount of property or gold he owns. Happiness or misery is in one's soul. A wise man feels at home in every country. The whole universe is the home of a noble soul.

—DEMOCRITUS

Nothing can give a man strength when he is looking for salvation other than his own effort.

May 8

There is nothing more attractive than humbleness and kindness. But you should not seek kindness which advertises itself.

A wise man said to another man who was chasing him, "If you have any grievance against me, tell me now, before we enter the city, otherwise other people will hear it and they will attack you."

—EGYPTIAN WISDOM

But he that is greatest among you, let him be as the younger; and he that is chief, as he that doth serve. For which is greater, he that sitteth at meat, or he that serveth? is not he that sitteth at meat? but I am among you as he that serveth.

—LUKE 22:26–27

The rivers and seas are the masters of the valleys across which they flow. This is because they are lower than the valleys. In the same way, a person who wants to be higher than other people should be lower than they; if he wants to guide people, he should be below them.

—LAO-TZU

A wise man was told that he was considered to be a bad person. He answered, "It is good that they do not know everything about me, because otherwise they could say worse things about me."

Try to avoid making judgments about yourself, especially by comparing yourself with others. Compare yourself only with perfection.

Life is constant change; it ought to consist of weakening the material and increasing the spiritual side of our existence.

Seek to learn constantly while you live; do not wait in the faith that old age by itself will bring wisdom.

—SOLON

Virtue always lasts longer than other qualities, and it always starts from the beginning.

—IMMANUEL KANT

The kindness of a dove is not virtue. A dove is not more virtuous than an eagle. Virtue begins only when there is an effort.

If God wanted to, he could have made us one nation, but he tests us. Wherever you go, in all places, try as much as you can to be kind, to be good, and then the day will come when God will unite all of us.

—The KORAN

We cannot stop on the way to self-perfection. As soon as you notice that you have a bigger interest in the outer world than in yourself, then you should know that the world moves behind you.

Only spiritual things exist in reality, and the material world is only an illusion.

If you want to save your soul, forget about your comfort.

May 10

Truly, only those things which are spiritual are real. Those things which can be seen and felt are only an illusion.

Life is given to us not only for pleasures.

—NIKOLAI GOGOL

No man can serve two masters; for either he will hate the one, and love the other; or else he will hold to the one, and despise the other. Ye cannot serve God and mammon.

—MATTHEW 6:24

In the long run, there is only one subject worthy of study, and this is the different forms of transformation of the spirit. All other subjects and studies can be brought to these basic things.

—HENRI AMIEL

I can send my thoughts to many different people at once; they will cross the seas and they will go to different lands if there is God's will, and the power of love and wisdom. My thoughts by themselves are a spiritual power; they can exist at the same time in thousands of places. My body, however, can only exist at one place at one time.

—LUCY MALORY

It seems to us that the most clear, understandable, and obviously existing things are not all there is. There is something else: unclear, unknown, contradictory, and nonexistent.

May 11

The moving force of all perfection, both for individuals and for whole nations, is not the understanding of what exists in this world, but the understanding of what can be achieved.

The weaker my hands, the more effort I should make to achieve perfection.

"You must be as perfect as your father in heaven."
 The perfection of the highest kindness is the goal for which all mankind strives. Christian learning about perfection is a tool for all mankind.

A person who sails far from the shore can see some shore-lines or cliffs. But when sailors go really far away from the shore, they can be guided only by the stars high up in the sky, and the compass which indicates their direction, and both these things are given to us.

No matter how low a person may fall, he will always be able to see that perfection toward which he should move.

May 12

Life is the constant approach to death; therefore, life can be bliss only when death does not seem to be an evil.

We say sometimes, "Here I will live in the rainy season, there I will live in the summer." So a crazy man dreams, because he does not think about death. But then death comes, and it takes all people with it: the man who is busy, and he who is concerned with something, and he who is greedy, and he who is absent-minded. Neither your son, nor your father, nor family or friends can help you when death comes. A wise man, one who understands this, looks for the way which leads to calmness.

—BUDDHIST WISDOM

A man comes into the world with his hands pushed into fists, as if he wants to say, "All this world is mine." A man leaves this world with his palms open, as if to say, "Look, I take nothing with me."

—The TALMUD

You should live your life as if you are ready to say good-bye to it at any moment, as if the time left you is some pleasant surprise.

—MARCUS AURELIUS

Your life is a small stretch of unlimited time. So have a good look at it, and make the best of it.

—SAID-BEN-HAMED

Remember, you do not live in the world, you only pass through it.

May 13

Every person should decide questions of life and death for himself.

A wise man sets requirements only for himself; an unwise man makes requirements for others.

—CHINESE WISDOM

A soul does not learn; it simply remembers what it knew all the time.

—DAUD EL GAFFER

A wise man always finds some support for himself in everything, because his gift is in obtaining goodness from everything.

—JOHN RUSKIN

Nothing will bring you peace except yourself.
—RALPH WALDO EMERSON

Only the truth which was acquired by your own thinking, through the efforts of your intellect, becomes a member of your own body, and only this truth really belongs to us.
—ARTHUR SCHOPENHAUER

May 14

The soul knows everything. No new thing can surprise it. Nothing can be bigger than it. Let others be afraid, but the soul is not afraid of anything. It lives according to its own laws. It is bigger than space and older than time. It gives courage against all the misfortunes of life.

—RALPH WALDO EMERSON

God lives in all people, but not all people live in God, and this is the source of their sufferings.

A lamp cannot burn without fire, and a person cannot live without God.

—THE GOSPEL OF SRI RAMAKRISHNA, a book of HINDUISM

Do you think that anybody can damage your soul? Then why are you so embarrassed? I laugh at those who think they can damage me. They do not know who I am, they do not know what I think, they cannot even touch the things which are really mine and with which I live.

—EPICTETUS

All things in the world belong to me. Creation and destruction happen according to my will. The present world is just a shell, and I am the yolk.

—PERSIAN WISDOM

The intellect questions, how and why? The dove does not ask, it says: I am love. It gives satisfaction without asking questions.

Fear nobody and nothing. That which is the most precious matter in you can be damaged by no one and by nothing.

Truth is not virtue, but the lack of vices.

The most common and the most widely used deceit is the wish to deceive not other people, but yourself. And this kind of life is the most harmful.

There are thousands of ways which lead to deception, and there is only one way which leads to the truth.
—Jean Jacques Rousseau

People should follow only the indisputable truth.
—Confucius

Truthfulness is the only real currency which circulates everywhere.
—Chinese proverb

Let us be truthful. This is the mystery of rhetoric and virtue, this is the biggest mystery, this is the highest achievement in art and the major law of life.
—Henri Amiel

One of the most common mistakes is to think that you can live without truth. The inner and outer consequences of even the smallest lies are usually more harmful than those small unpleasant things which result from telling the truth directly.

May 16

Humanity has never lived and cannot live without religion.

Religion is the necessity and prime condition of the life of an intellectual person.

The stronger the religious feeling is, the better one understands what is and what should be the guide of all one's actions.

It is difficult enough to plug your ears in a big hall full of dancing people; now imagine that you are in an asylum. For one who destroys in himself his religious conscience, all of the religious activity of other people will produce a similar impression. But it is dangerous to think that you are more clever than the majority of religious mankind.

—HENRI AMIEL

People often say that religion loses its power amidst humanity. This is not true, and this cannot be true. This happens because the people who think so observe only a small group of people, and there are always certain people who do not have religious feelings.

If a person has problems, there can be only one root cause: lack of faith. The same is true within human societies as a whole.

May 17

The greatest joy, according to the works of Francis Assisi, is that you can endure everything, you can even suffer slander and physical pain, and at the end you are able to feel no animosity toward these sufferings, but you feel joy, because you have faith; such joy cannot be destroyed, either by evil people or by your own suffering.

The quality of a really virtuous person is to be unknown to people, or to be misunderstood by people, but not to be disappointed by this.

—CHINESE WISDOM

When they blame you and scold you and discuss you, then you should rejoice; when they praise you and admire you, then you should be sad.

Libel and a false reputation which you can destroy is the best school of goodness.

The blaming and criticism of other people is bad. But at the same time it is understandable, and it is valuable as the only test of your love for God and your neighbor.

May 18

One cannot say that the understanding of the divine essence of your soul gives you power, for this understanding raises you to that level which transcends any notions of force or weakness and therefore of power.

Heaven is closer to those people who purify their souls. Those who have only the knowledge received by our five senses do not know the essence of things. The real knowledge is the understanding that there is a higher spiritual force.

—INDIAN WISDOM

People may ask you, "Why do you know God?" You should respond, "Because he is in my heart." Look at the essence of life, not with the eyes in your head, but with the eyes of your heart. Can you know yourself, if you do not know God? The real understanding of yourself is the understanding of God.

—PERSIAN WISDOM

Who can harm you, who can be more powerful than you, if you are united with God? And can do this.

May 19

The foundation of all faiths is the same.

It only seems that people are busy with trade, with making agreements, negotiations and wars, science and the arts. There is in fact only one thing which people do; this is to search for the understanding of the moral law by which they live. And this understanding is not only the most important but the only real concern for all humankind.

A wise man was asked, "Is there a single word which you can follow throughout all your life?" And the wise man answered, "There is such a word. This is *shu*." And the meaning of this word is, "If we do not want certain things to be done to us, we should not do such things to others."

—CHINESE WISDOM

You should behave in such a way that you can say to everybody, "Behave as I do."

—After IMMANUEL KANT

The really true and unchanging law, that law which gives us true direction and which forbids us to do bad things, is the intellect of a higher, superior being.

—MARCUS TULLIUS CICERO

When you clash with other people, remember the law of reciprocity. You should do to others those things which you want done to you. This should become your way of life.

May 20

For a person, for an animal, indeed for any living being, there is neither logic nor meaning in the word "freedom" because all our lives are limited by many constraints. And yet if a person understands himself as a spiritual being, he cannot even speak about not being free: the idea of not being free cannot be applied to the notions of intellect, conscience, and love.

Remember that your understanding of your inner self holds the meaning of your life, and it makes you free if you do not force it to serve your flesh. The human soul which is enlightened by understanding and freed from passions, and lit with the divine light, stands on a firm foundation.

And ye shall know the truth, and the truth shall make you free.
—JOHN 8:32

Evil does not exist in material nature by itself, but evil exists for every person who understands goodness, and who has the freedom of choice between good and bad.
—MARCUS AURELIUS

We understand very clearly that to be a person with high morals is to be a person with a liberated soul. Those who are disappointed or concerned or afraid, or who are involved in passions, cannot free their souls.
—CONFUCIUS

People who deny freedom remind me of blind people who deny colors. They do not know the nature of freedom.

May 21

In order to live in goodness, try doing it.

You should celebrate each new day with a good action, a good deed. This is the best way to start a new day.

Nobody has any idea about what goodness is, until they start doing it.

—HARRIET MARTINEAU

God's love will go from heaven to those who give to the poor. A double blessing will go to those who, while doing this, meet the poor and tenderly say "good-bye" to them.

—The TALMUD

When you do a good deed, be grateful that you have had the chance to do it.

You must know firmly and feel deeply that you should dedicate every day to the good of your fellows, doing everything you can for them. You have to do it and not talk about it.

—JOHN RUSKIN

If you cannot teach yourself to seek possibilities for doing good and to do good at every possible occasion, then at least do not miss a chance to do good.

May 22

The greatest changes in the world are made slowly and gradually, not with eruptions and revolutions.

The same things happen in one's spiritual life.

All great thoughts are living thoughts, and they can grow and be changed. And they change and grow as a tree, and not as a cloud.

—JOHN RUSKIN

All really great things are happening in slow and inconspicuous ways.

The process of life should be the birth of a soul. This is the highest alchemy, and this justifies our presence on earth. This is our calling and our virtue.

—HENRI AMIEL

Our life is unceasing wonder, growth, and development.

—LUCY MALORY

There is nothing more harmful for your inner perfection than the understanding that you are doing well. The way to happiness, the way to real moral improvement, moves so invisibly, so inconspicuously, that a person can see his successes only after great, lengthy periods of time.

If you think that you are moving toward perfection and you notice this, then you should know that you are mistaken, that you have stopped and are moving backward.

May 23

We should be satisfied with the small things in life. The less we need, the less trouble we can have.

It is a great happiness to have what you desire; but it is an even greater happiness not to want more than you already have.

—MENEDEMUS

Who is a wise man?—He who studies all the time.
Who is strong?—He who can limit himself.
Who is rich?—He who is happy with what he has.

—The TALMUD

Nature needs small things, but your imagination needs much.

From pleasures appear sadness and fear. He who is free from pleasures does not have either fear or sadness.

—BUDDHIST WISDOM

The initial joy on becoming free is better than being a king; it is more beautiful than going to heaven; it is more important than commanding whole worlds.

—BUDDHIST WISDOM

The growth of your desires is not the way to perfection, as many people think. To the contrary, the more a person limits himself, the better he can understand his human dignity, and the more free, the more brave he becomes, and most importantly, the more capable of serving God and other people.

May 24

Love is one of the manifestations of God in man.

The purpose of life is to express love in all its manifestations.

In order to be happy, you should love—love with self-sacrifice, love all and everything, and spread a network of love everywhere. No matter who gets into this net, catch them all and fill them with love.

Everyone can recall a moment, universal to all, perhaps from early childhood, when you wanted to love everyone and everything—your father, your mother, your brothers, evil people, a dog, a cat, grass—and you wanted everyone to feel good, everyone to feel happy; and even more, you wanted to do something special so that everyone would be happy, even to sacrifice yourself, to give your life so that everyone should feel happy and joyful. This feeling is the feeling of love, and it must be returned to, for it is the life of every person.

Anything you do should be filled with love.

May 25

You should be careful not to follow bad examples. When you hear your neighbor slandering others, try to stop him.
—From the BOOK OF DIVINE THOUGHTS

There is no worse harm for a person with a strong intellect than the temptation to make witty remarks that blame and mock his neighbors.

Making jokes and blaming and mocking others is like covering a dead body with a nice sauce and presenting it as a meal. Without the sauce, you would turn away, but with it, you find you can easily eat this distasteful meal.

Never listen to those who blame others and speak well about you.

You have to think about what you say; only then will you feel quiet and kind and filled with love. The more you are irritated, the more excited you become, the more care you must exercise not to sin with your words by abusing others.

The manner of one's death can be in accord with the manner of one's life, and therefore it can be a moral action. An animal simply dies, but a human should return his soul to its creator.

—HENRI AMIEL

Christ's greatest words were said immediately before his death, when he forgave his persecutors, who did not understand what they did. The words and actions of a dying person have great power over people, and thus it is important both to live a good life and to die in a good way. A good death takes away the sins of a bad life.

During the minutes of death, a person can see a candle, in the light of which he reads the book of a life filled with problems, lies, evils, and misfortunes. And, in the minutes of dying, this candle lights up all the world with a very bright and clear light, and brightens up all the corners of a person's life, even those corners which were always covered with darkness; and then it makes some slight noise, and the light goes down and disappears forever.

When you get ready to die, do not worry about the usual things, like following rituals or taking care of everyday business. Be prepared so that you can die in the best way possible. Use all the mighty influence of those powerful strong minutes of death, when a person exists partially in the other world, and his words and deeds have special power over those who remain in this world.

Very often, all of the activity of the human mind is directed not in revealing the truth, but in hiding the truth. The potential of the human mind to act this way is our major source of temptation.

The court jury has, as its raison d'être, the task of preserving society as it exists now, and therefore, it persecutes and executes those who stand higher than the general level of society, and it serves those who are lower than the general level.

A man cannot do everything; but this cannot be an excuse for doing bad things.

—HENRY DAVID THOREAU

I love peasants and farmers; they are not scholarly enough nor educated enough to tell sophisticated lies.

—CHARLES DE MONTESQUIEU

If you see that an action is explained by a very sophisticated reasoning, then you can be sure that this action is bad. The decisions of the conscience are always strict and simple.

May 28

For the pagan world, a man's richness indicates his glory and importance; in a truly Christian world, the great wealth of a man is an indication of his weakness and lies.

People are so involved in their material interests that when they look at the manifestations of the human soul, and at pure relationships between people, they look at them from the point of view of how to improve their material well-being. Respectability is often measured by one's wealth, and not by his real inner spiritual value.

—After RALPH WALDO EMERSON

The possession of great wealth is a school of pride, cruelty, self-admiration, and dissipation.

The lack of sensitivity among rich people is not as cruel as their compassion.

—After JEAN JACQUES ROUSSEAU

You should not respect poor people too much, but you should take pity on them. A rich person should not be proud of his wealth; he should be ashamed of it.

Life is the understanding of a holy spirit in yourself; a holy spirit which is put into some limits.

The only clear and final truth is the truth of conscience.
—RENÉ DESCARTES

Under my feet, there is cold frozen earth; around me huge trees are standing; above my head is the foggy cold sky. I feel my body, I feel my mind occupied with various thoughts. And at the same time I know that all these things, all this frosted cold earth, and the trees, and the sky, and my body, and my thoughts, this is all created by chance, this is a temporary world, the creation of my five senses. The world created by me exists only because I am part of it, and therefore, I separate myself from the world. I know that I could die, but the world will not disappear.

Death will make some changes in me, and while I will not be completely destroyed, I will become another being, separate from this world. Now, at present, I understand myself; then, something different altogether will happen to my inner self. And there can be a limitless number of such beings, which exist separately from this world.

Our life is our limited understanding of this eternal and limitless spirit which knows no constraints in time and space and which is not bound by any spatial or timely events.

The human conscience is a divine conscience.

May 30

Our land, like our character, cannot be the object of buying and selling. Behind the buying and selling of earth is the hidden process of buying and selling a personality.

Earth is the great gift which nature gave to people, and the birth of every person in this world should give him the right to possess this earth. And this right should be as natural as the right of a person to have the breast of his mother.

—JEAN FRANÇOIS MARMONTEL

A person in our society cannot sleep without paying for the place where he sleeps; he has the right to have free air or water or sunlight only when he is on the road. The only right he has is to walk along this road; until he becomes tired, or he cannot walk, he has to continue walking.

The bodies of men and women, and even more importantly, their children, should not be bought and sold. So too the water, the land and air, because these things are necessary conditions of this existence.

—JOHN RUSKIN

People strive in this world, not for those things which are truly good, but for the possession of many things which they can call their property.

May 31

A person who is not used to luxury, but who acquired luxury quite by chance, often pretends, in order to become more important in his own eyes and in the eyes of other people, that luxury is natural for him, that he is not surprised by it, that he neglects it. In the same way a stupid person pretends that he is bored with life, and that he can find something more interesting.

The joy of your spirit is the indication of your strength.
—Ralph Waldo Emerson

You must believe in the possibility of happiness in order to be happy.

Take from a person who follows the divine law everything which other people think of as comfort and wealth, and nevertheless such a person will remain happy.

A person who has spoiled his stomach will criticize his meals saying that the food is bad; the same thing happens with people who are not satisfied with their lives in this world.

We do not have the right to be unhappy with our life. If it seems to us that we are not satisfied with life, we should see this as a reason to be unsatisfied with ourselves.

Better to do nothing than to do harm.

We often refuse to participate in the innocent joys of life because we are too busy with something we feel we have to do. We should accept these moments, because the sweet and joyful game is sometimes more important and necessary than most other things. Very often the business which busy people claim to be doing is not important at all, and sometimes it would be better left undone.

Cruel people are busy all the time, as if to find justification for the cruelty of their dealings.

It is a common misconception to think that pleasures and joys are unimportant and sometimes evil; as for example, Islam, or ancient old Orthodox Christianity, or Puritanism would have it. Pleasure is as important as work, and is the reward of work. Work cannot last endlessly, and the necessary rest should usually conclude with some period of pleasure.

Pleasures are only bad in these three cases: when we have to make other people work for us because it is impossible for us to satisfy our desire for pleasures, when we plan competitive games to determine who will have the best or the most pleasures, and when pleasures are allowed only for selected people. But if these evils are avoided, then pleasure, especially for young people, is not an evil, but a good.

Work and pleasure should be alternated, one after the other; they fill our lives with joy, though not every work and every pleasure can do this.

June 2

For whosoever exalteth himself shall be abased; and he that humbleth himself shall be exalted.

—LUKE 14:11

A person who stands on his tiptoes cannot stand long, and a person who is too proud of himself cannot set a good example.

—LAO-TZU

He who is looking for wisdom is already wise; and he who thinks that he has found wisdom is a stupid man.

—EASTERN WISDOM

No exterior force can make you humble. There is only one way to be humble: do not think about yourself, but about how you can serve God and others.

June 3

Whether they know it or not, all creatures are inseparably connected.

I will never seek or accept merely my own personal salvation. I do not want to receive satisfaction by myself; always and everywhere I live and work, I will hope and strive for the universal salvation of all people and all creatures in the world. Until all have been saved and freed, I will not abandon this world of sin, sadness, and strife.

—ANCIENT CHINESE WISDOM

Understand that you are part of a great spiritual brotherhood; there is something cheering and soothing in the thought which will make you calm and satisfied.

—MARCUS AURELIUS

Humanity has begun to understand that we will all rise or fall together—that we are bound together, as we live together. People are listening more and more to the voice which speaks this inside of us.

—LUCY MALORY

Individual goodness and individual evil both have the power to spread goodness or evil throughout the world.

June 4

Due to the current distortion, perversion, and false understanding of Christianity, our lives have become worse than those of pagans.

A man should be a servant, and he should make a choice of whose servant he is: if he is the servant of his passions, then he is a servant of other human beings, but if he is the servant of his inner divine spirit, then he is a servant of God alone.

It is better to have a superior master.

The salvation of mankind depends upon independent thinkers directing their thoughts rightly.

—RALPH WALDO EMERSON

The more respect that different objects, customs, or laws are given, the more attentively you have to question the right these things have to this respect.

Uprooting the existing evils of this life can begin only by making our religions open, so that every single human being in the world can reveal religious life and can discuss and create and discover religious truth.

If we say that the outer world exists only as we see it, we deny that there are other beings, with senses different from our own.

When I cast my gaze on objects, I try to correlate their outlines with ideas that already exist in my head. I will see white on the horizon, and I will think, There is a white church in the distance. Do we not give everything we see in this world a preexisting form from our imagination, brought by us from our previous life?

We can see that all of the world's objects exist in two ways: in relation to their place and time—by understanding that they exist in God and were created by the same Divine Nature which every spiritual thing in this world bears in relation to eternity.

—After BENEDICTUS SPINOZA

In reality, the outer world in itself is not as we see it, and thus everything material in this world is insignificant. What is important then? That thing which exists everywhere, at all times, and for all people: the divine spark, the spiritual root of our lives.

An evil deed not only destroys the soul but often returns to bring evil on the evildoer.

The greatest virtue is to do no evil, even to your enemies. If you respect yourself, you will not commit evil, even in the slightest way.

—INDIAN WISDOM

When you throw a ball up in the air, it doesn't stay there but returns to the earth; likewise all your good or bad actions will return to you in another form, according to the desire of your heart, no matter which path you take.

—BUDDHIST WISDOM

An evildoer is happy while the evil is not yet ripe, but when it is ripe and ready, he will understand what evil is, and his evil will return to him like dust thrown against the wind.

Neither in the sky nor in the earth nor in the depth of mountains, nor anywhere in this world is there a place where one can escape the results of sin.

—DHAMMAPADA, a book of BUDDHIST WISDOM

A person who broods on revenge only worsens his wounds. His injuries would heal if he would refrain.

—FRANCIS BACON

Sinning is as dangerous as irritating a wild beast. In most cases in this world, evil returns to the evildoer in the worst and rudest form.

June 7

Calmness and humility provide pleasures which are not accessible to the selfish and the proud.

The prerequisite of a good life is peace between people, and the major obstacle to peace is pride. A person should be humble, prepared to be falsely accused, ready for everything; only then can he bring peace into his relationships and into the lives of others.

Come unto me, all ye that labor and are heavy laden and I will give you rest. Take my yoke upon you, and learn of me; for I am meek and lowly in heart: and ye shall find rest unto your souls. For my yoke is easy, and my burden is light.

—MATTHEW 11:28–30

Pride defends itself, and not only itself but other sins, and it hates humility, so it rejects the cure, and hides and justifies the sin. The understanding of sin has a positive influence on a person; it is even more useful than a good deed, which can increase pride.

Be strict in judging yourself and gentle in judging others, and you will have no enemies.

—CHINESE WISDOM

Do not be afraid to be humiliated if you can accept this with humility—you will be repaid many times in the spiritual blessings which are connected with being humble.

June 8

Without truth there is no kindness; without kindness the truth cannot be told.

And why call ye me, Lord, Lord, and do not the things which I say? Whosoever cometh to me, and heareth my sayings, and doeth them, I will shew you to whom he is like: He is like a man which built an house, and digged deep, and laid the foundation on a rock: and when the flood arose, the stream beat vehemently upon that house and could not shake it: for it was founded upon a rock. But he that heareth, and doeth not, is like a man that without a foundation built an house upon the earth; against which the stream did beat vehemently, and immediately it fell; and the ruin of that house was great.

—LUKE 6:46–49

Always respond to hatred with kindness. The most difficult enterprises are easiest at their inception, and the greatest of enterprises have humble origins. Confront difficulties while they are still easy, then, and tackle a big thing when it is still small.

—LAO-TZU

There are two paths which lead to virtue: the first is to be truthful and just, and the second is to do no evil to living beings.

—MANU

Disguising yourself as a kind person is worse than being nakedly mean.

Christian society, as it now exists, doesn't follow Christian law in its real meaning.

Almost every effort of the human mind is directed, not toward lightening the work of the laborer, but toward making more pleasant the idleness of the leisured.

If a person could look at our world from a distance he would see so much stupidity and hatred that he would probably cry. We do so many funny and stupid and impoverished hateful deeds. One person hunts wild animals and becomes an animal himself; another feeds donkeys and horses to carry loads, and despises people who die of hunger. Other people spend a great deal of money to create huge houses and do nothing to help the homeless. Some people seek only profits, others spend only for dissipation, and others steal.

In all of these excesses, all of this criminal behavior, we see people who only want to take care of themselves, without a thought about what is most necessary in this world.

—Saint John Chrysostom

It defies the laws of nature for a child to rule an adult, or a fool to guide a wise man. Likewise, it is against the law of nature that a small group of people should be overindulged when a huge, hungry crowd's most basic needs aren't met.

There is only one thing in this world which is worth dedicating all your life. This is creating more love among people and destroying barriers which exist between them.

June 10

There is something in the soul which cannot die, which cannot be affected by death.

He who defeats others is strong; he who defeats himself is powerful, and he who knows when he dies that he will not be destroyed is eternal.

—LAO-TZU

People are born and live only as manifestations, or pieces of God; therefore they cannot be completely destroyed. They can disappear from before our eyes, but they cannot be destroyed. One person was within my sight for a long time; another went out of my sight very quickly; but I cannot say that the first person existed more and the second less. It doesn't matter whether a man passes by my window quickly or slowly. I know definitely that this man existed in the time before I saw him and that he will exist in the time after he has disappeared from my sight.

He who knows that the foundation of this life is spirit is out of danger. When he closes the gates of his senses at the end of his life, he has no troubles.

—After LAO-TZU

Real life exists outside time and space; therefore, death can change the manifestation of life in this world, but it cannot destroy life itself.

Try to live with the part of your soul which understands eternity, which is not afraid of death. And that part of your soul is love.

June 11

All material changes in our everyday life are small in comparison with those in our spiritual life. There could be a change in feelings and actions, there could be a change in thoughts and ideas. In order to change your thoughts and ideas, you should concentrate your conscious mind on your spiritual requirements.

Every thought a person dwells upon, whether he expresses it or not, either damages or improves his life.

—LUCY MALORY

To vanquish sin, you must accept that the root of each sin is in a bad thought. We are all only the consequences of what we think.

—BUDDHA

We regret losing a purse full of money, but a good thought which has come to us, which we've heard or read, a thought which we should have remembered and applied to our life, which could have improved the world—we lose this thought and promptly forget about it, and we do not regret it, though it is more precious than millions.

June 12

Suffering is the necessary condition for spiritual and physical growth.

Really, really I tell you, you will cry, and you will fall, and the world will be glorified. You will be sad, and your sadness will become joy. A woman is in pain when she gives birth to a child, and after the birth she doesn't remember, and she is joyful.

—JOHN 16:20–21

Very often we say that we don't like suffering, that we have too much suffering, but sufferings, all kinds of sufferings, are always good for us. Sometimes, we even see that it is useful to suffer: children suffer when they grow, or when it is necessary that they clean an injury filled with filth. We cannot see the usefulness of moral sufferings, but those sufferings, too, make us better and closer to God.

We grow thus: We come closer to God and God comes closer to us as our will becomes united with the will of God.

—RALPH WALDO EMERSON

You should look in suffering for the seeds of your future spiritual growth, or the bitterness of suffering will be severe.

June 13

Intellect is the quality that makes us different from animals.

Buddha said: "In meditation, in speech, in life, in studies, I never forget about the most important thing: the requirements of the intellect."

The moral and the intellectual are always in harmony.

If a self-confident man talks to a wise man, he will not understand the truth, just as a spoon will not understand the truth when it gets into the mouth.

—EASTERN WISDOM

I cannot cause any improvement in anyone except with the help of the goodness and kindness which already is inherent in this person.

—IMMANUEL KANT

People spoil their life who neglect their intellect and say that it cannot guide them.

Intellect is the same in all people, and communication is based on intellect; therefore every man must correspond to its requirements.

When you make an effort not to blame other people, your life becomes much easier, but very few people make this small effort.

In the lives of the saints, there is the story of the hermit who saw in his dream a monk who had died long ago, and who had been rather weak in his life. The monk was in an especially lovely and honored part of paradise. The hermit asked, "How were you granted this place, with all your weaknesses?" and the monk answered that it was because he had never blamed, not a single person in his life.

Therefore thou art inexcusable, O man, whosoever thou art that judgest: for wherein thou judgest another, thou condemnest thyself; for thou that judgest doest the same things.

—ROMANS 2:1

The more strictly and mercilessly you judge yourself, the more just and kind you will be in the judgment of others.
—CONFUCIUS

Do not glorify in blaming and despising other people. A kind person should hide the shame of others, even those who have harmed him. Do not remember one who repents his former sins.

—The TALMUD

Unless you yourself are sinless, do not say a single word about the sins of others, but be quiet. If you make it a habit not to blame others, you will feel the growth of the ability to love in your soul, and you will see the growth of goodness in your life.

To love God means to love the highest possible good which we can imagine in all things.

People often say, "I do not understand love of God; what is love of God?" It would be more exact to say, "cannot understand love in this world without love of God."

Real love of God is a moral feeling based on a clear understanding of His high, superior being; love of God coincides with love of virtue, truth, and kindness.

—WILLIAM ELLERY CHANNING

A person who understands the law but who is far from the love of God is like a bank official who has keys for the inside of his building but not the key for the front door.

—The TALMUD

The commandments of God should be followed because of love of God, not because of fear of God.

—The TALMUD

If you love a person without loving God, which is the goodness inside of him, then you plant the seeds for future disappointments and sufferings with this love.

Those who say that they love God but dislike their neighbors are lying to people; those who love their neighbors but don't love God are lying to themselves.

Only perfection is worth complete love. In order to feel complete love, we can either delude ourselves that some imperfect object of our love is "perfection" or we can love perfection, which is God.

June 16

The improvement of society can be achieved only by the moral improvement of individuals.

We live in an epoch of discipline, culture, and civilization, but not in an epoch of morality. In the present state, we can say that the happiness of the people grows, and yet the unhappiness of the people increases as well. How can we make people happy when they are not educated to have high morals? They do not become wise.

—IMMANUEL KANT

There can be only one way to fight the general evil of life: it is in the moral, religious, and spiritual perfection of your own life.

The misfortunes of war and preparations for war bear little relation to the reasons given to explain war: the real reasons are usually so insignificant that they are not even worth discussion, and they are completely unknown to those who die.

The madness of contemporary war is justified by dynastic interest, common nationalism, European equilibrium, or ambitions. If there are ambitions in people, this is a very strange way to sustain it, with all the crimes which happen to people during war: destruction of homes, plunder, and mass murder.

—ANATOLE FRANCE

You ask me, is it necessary for civilized people to make war? And I tell you not only is it "already" unnecessary, but it was never necessary, and not sometimes but always it destroys the normal development of humanity, destroys justice, and stops progress.

—GALSTON MOHK

Only during a period of war does it become obvious how millions of people can be manipulated. People, millions of people, are filled with pride while doing things which those same people actually consider stupid, evil, dangerous, painful, and criminal, and they strongly criticize these things—but continue doing them.

The reasons which governments give for wars are always screens, behind which lie completely different reasons and motives.

June 18

Understanding our duty provides us with the understanding of our divine soul. And, too, the understanding of our divine soul gives us the understanding of duty.

There is in our soul something that, if we see it as it is and give it the proper attention, will always give us great pleasure; this something is the moral disposition or quality which was given to us at our creation.

—IMMANUEL KANT

People can reach heavenly joy: those pure ones who are filled with the desire for a good life receive pleasures in their body, in their material life. When your mind and your heart are pure, then the divine will be opened for you.

—BRAHMIN INDIAN WISDOM

If your heart is filled with virtue, then you will find happiness and beauty.

—RALPH WALDO EMERSON

The voice of your conscience is the voice of God.

Your conscience is your understanding of your spiritual origins; only when you possess such awareness will it be a real guide in your life.

There are two different beings within you, one which is blind and sensual, and another which can see and is spiritual.

This spiritual being is called conscience and can be compared with the needle of a compass which points at goodness at one end, and at the other, evil. We cannot perceive this compass until we stray from goodness, but as soon as we do something bad, then we feel this pull away from the direction of goodness in life.

God gave us the consciousness of mankind as a whole, as well as our own consciousness as individuals; with the help of these two things, as with two wings we can fly higher and come closer to God and to understand the truth.

—GIUSEPPE MAZZINI

Oh, conscience: you are the deathless voice of heaven, and a true guide and judge of goodness. You make a person resemble God.

—JEAN JACQUES ROUSSEAU

Youth is the time of passions and infatuations, and yet listen now to the voice of your conscience and accept it as the greatest authority. Always ask yourself, do my actions coincide with my conscience? And do not be afraid to arrive at meanings different from other people's.

—THEODORE PARKER

Fear all that is not accepted by your conscience.

June 20

There was a time when people ate human flesh and found nothing wrong in it; even now there are such wild people. People stopped eating human meat, little by little; now they cease to eat the meat of animals little by little, though it has taken time. *But the time will come when people will have the same disgust for the meat of animals as they now have for human flesh.*

—After ALPHONSE LAMARTINE

It is terrible to throw little children to other people as foundlings, to organize gladiators' fights, to torture prisoners, and to do other such uncivilized deeds. In the future, the time will come when it will be unacceptable to kill animals and take their dead bodies as your food.

—DR. JOHANN GEORG VON ZIMMERMANN

Do not raise your hand against your brother, and do not spill the blood of any living creatures who live on this earth, neither human beings nor pets nor wild animals nor birds. In the depth of your soul some divine voice stops you from spilling this blood. There is life in it. You cannot return this life.

—ALPHONSE LAMARTINE

In our time, the killing of animals for pleasure or food is almost a crime, and hunting and eating meat are not just trivial things, but bad actions, which like any other bad actions lead to many other actions which are worse.

June 21

The misery of the unintellectual life brings us to the need for an intellectual life.

Before, I lived in sin, and I saw that the majority of people around me lived in the same way. Like a robber, I knew I was unhappy and I suffered, and that people around me were unhappy and they suffered; and I didn't see any way out of this situation except for suicide or death. Life seemed terrible to me. And then I heard the words of Christ and I understood them. And life ceased to seem an evil, and instead of desperation I felt a happiness for life which surpasses even death.

We can understand wisdom in three ways: first, by meditation; this is the most noble way. Secondly, by being influenced by someone or following someone; this is the easiest way. Third is the way of experience; this is the most difficult way.

—CONFUCIUS

When you suffer, think not on how you can escape suffering, but concentrate your efforts on what kind of inner moral and spiritual perfection this suffering requires.

All the misfortunes of mankind collectively and individually are not useless; they bring people and individuals and nations in different ways closer to the purpose which is set before them: the appearance of God, for every person in himself, and in all mankind.

There is only one true religion for all of mankind.

The difference between religions—what a strange expression. Certainly there can be different faiths, and beliefs in historical events which are passed from one generation to another to strengthen religion; in the same way there can be different religious books—the Sutras, Vedas, Koran, etc. But there can be only one religion, and it is real for all times.

—IMMANUEL KANT

We can believe in a thing, we can know that it exists, even if we cannot understand it with our intellect, or explain it with words.

If you are a Muslim, go and live as a Christian; if you are a Christian live as a Jew; if you are Catholic, live as an Orthodox—whatever religion you have, hold the same respect for people of different religions. If your speech together does not arouse or excite you to indignation and if you can freely communicate with them, you have achieved peace. It is said that the object of every religion is the same: all people look for love, and all the world is a place of love. Then why should we speak about the difference between the Muslim church and the Christian church?

—ISLAMIC WISDOM

Do not fear hesitations but study the different faiths and religions intellectually.

Only he who accepts that the essence or meaning of his life is not material but spiritual can be free.

A slave who is happy with his state is a slave twice over, because not only his body but his soul is enslaved.

O God, while I stay on this earth I want to be that which I am.

—EPICTETUS

Peace is a great blessing if it can be reached, but if peace is reached by slavery, it becomes a misfortune and not a blessing. Peace is the freedom which is based on the acceptance of every person's rights, and slavery is the negation of rights, and of human dignity. Therefore, we should sacrifice everything to achieve peace, but even more, to get rid of slavery.

—After MARCUS TULLIUS CICERO

Remember that you are more free if you change your opinion and follow those who have corrected your mistakes, than if you are stubborn about your mistakes.

—MARCUS AURELIUS

There is only one real knowledge: that which helps us to be free. Every other type of knowledge is mere amusement.

—VISHNU PURANA, INDIAN WISDOM

There is no middle way: either be a slave of people or of God.

Understanding or mindfulness of death teaches one to choose the things which are complete or could be completed; and those things are the most important.

You could die very quickly; but yet you have time to rid yourself of your passions. Be humble to everyone.

—MARCUS AURELIUS

A wise person thinks more about life than about death.

—BENEDICTUS SPINOZA

There is no death for the spirit; therefore, a person who lives a spiritual life is freed from death.

Do you worry about the moment when you die? Our life is only a moment in eternity. Think and you will see that you have eternity behind you and before you, and between these two huge abysses, what difference does it make whether you live three days or three centuries?

—MARCUS AURELIUS

Whenever you ask whether you should behave in this way or the other, ask yourself, what would you do if you knew that you could die this evening, and nobody would find out about your action? Death spurs people to finish their affairs; among all actions, there is only one type which is complete, and that is love which seeks no reward.

June 25

It is very useful to notice the impression which our life and deeds make upon other people.

You should live so that other people think well of you and you think well of yourself.

—LUCY MALORY

The very shortcomings which make others difficult and unbearable mean less in yourself. You do not see them, and when you speak of other people having these drawbacks, you do not notice that you are describing yourself.

—JEAN DE LA BRUYÈRE

The simplest, quickest, and surest means to becoming known as a virtuous person is to work on yourself, to actually be virtuous. Examine each virtue, and you will see that they all were achieved with work and exercise.

—SOCRATES

One man keeps silence, and people discuss him. Another speaks a lot, and people discuss him. A third speaks a little, and people discuss him. There is no such thing as a person who is not being discussed or scolded.

—DHAMMAPADA, a book of BUDDHIST WISDOM

Do you call a person happy if he finds his strength in his children or in his friends, or in other things which are impermanent? In one second, his prosperity can be ruined. Seek no other support than your inner self and God.

—DEMOSTHENES

Never try to justify your deeds.

June 26

Love provides a person with the purpose of his life. Intellect shows him the means to achieve that purpose.

In the scheme of the world, a person is no more than a pine cone, or a weak herb, or a bit of swamp grass, but he is a grass which possesses some intellect.

—BLAISE PASCAL

Man differs from other animals only in his intellect; some people try to develop it and others neglect it, just as they try to reject those other qualities which differentiate them from the animals.

—EASTERN WISDOM

I praise Christianity because it develops, strengthens, and elevates my intellectual nature.

—WILLIAM ELLLERY CHANNING

If a person lacks intellect, he can not distinguish bad from good, and so he can neither truly seek nor truly have real goodness.

A good life is given only to those who make efforts to achieve it.

In order to have a good life, you should not be afraid of any good deeds. You should have no less power or strength for small acts than for the biggest and greatest good deed.

In order not to pour out a vessel full of water, you should hold it evenly. In order to have a razor sharp, you should sharpen it. The same should happen with your soul if you are looking for real goodness.

—LAO-TZU

If there is something great in you, it will not appear on your first call. It will not appear and come to you easily, without any work and effort.

—RALPH WALDO EMERSON

Ask, and it shall be given you; seek, and ye shall find; knock, and it shall be opened unto you: for every one that asketh receiveth; and he that seeketh findeth; and to him that knocketh it shall be opened.

—MATTHEW 7:7–8

Try to live a good life in accord with the virtues that are set before you. Perhaps this is a difficult thing, but with time it becomes more and more joyful.

If you need goodness, follow God's law. And to follow the law of God is possible only by making an effort. Not only is this effort rewarded with a happy life, but even the effort itself gives the biggest blessing of life.

June 28

The family relationship is only good and firm and giving of virtue to people when it goes beyond family and is also religious, and all the members of the family believe in one God and His law. Otherwise, the family is the source not of pleasure but of suffering.

One of the most common explanations for bad deeds is the family name. People steal, make bribes, do many other nasty things in life, all of which can be explained by their love for their family.

Family love is a selfish feeling, and therefore it can justify bad, unworthy actions.

And it was told him by certain, which said, Thy mother and thy brethren stand without, desiring to see thee. And he answered and said unto them, My mother and my brethren are these which hear the word of God, and do it.

—LUKE 8:20–21

He that loveth father or mother more than me is not worthy of me: and he that loveth son or daughter more than me is not worthy of me.

—MATTHEW 10:37

In family love, in the moral high meaning, there is nothing good or bad, just as in self-love. Both are natural. Love of your family, as well as of yourself, when it surpasses its limits, can be a vice, but it can never be a virtue, because it's a natural feeling.

June 29

Depression is a state of the soul in which you can see no sense either in your own life or in the life of the world. This state is not only painful for the people around you, but it can influence them, and a truly good person deals with this unpleasantness when he is alone. When you have bad spirits or are in a low mood, or you are irritated, you should be so in solitude.

When everything you see appears in dark, gloomy shades, and seems baleful, and you want to tell others only bad and unpleasant things, do not trust your perceptions. Treat yourself as though you were drunk. Take no steps and actions until this state has disappeared.

You should never feel depressed.

A man should always feel happy; if he is unhappy, it means he is guilty.

O Lord, help me to be always happy and to rejoice following and fulfilling your will.

Both our physical sufferings and periods of depression are part of our life in this world, and we should patiently wait until they are over, or our life is over.

June 30

As soon as a person asks himself the question, "How do I live my life in the best way?" then all other questions are answered.

Real living takes place not in the domain of outward change, but in the inner domain, where changes can hardly be observed, in our spiritual life.

And Jesus answered and said unto her, Martha, Martha, thou art careful and troubled about many things: But one thing is needful: and Mary hath chosen that good part, which shall not be taken away from her.

—LUKE 10:41–42

Instead of saving humanity, every person should save himself.

—ALEXANDER HERZEN

The more people believe that others can improve their lives, the slower any improvement will occur.

July 1

The human soul is divine.

Every truth has its origin in God. When it is manifested in a man, this is not because it comes from him, but because he has such a quantity of transparency that he can reveal it.

—BLAISE PASCAL

When after the rain, water flows from the roof through pipes, it seems to us that water flows out of these pipes, but in reality, it falls from the sky. The same phenomenon can be seen with the religious teachings taught to us by holy people. It seems to us that this teaching comes from them, but in reality, these teachings come from God.

—THE GOSPEL OF SRI RAMAKRISHNA

A person's purpose on this earth is to be in harmony with eternity. It is only then that the universal flow of love and intellect can be channeled through this person, as if through a clear pathway.

—LUCY MALORY

Life is given to us in the same way as a child is given to a nanny, so that it can be raised to maturity.

Keep yourself in purity, far from evil, so that divine power may come through you. And in this flow of divine power through you, there is great bliss.

July 2

There is no other domain where the words of our language are so misused as in the criticism of art, especially of false art.

A work of art makes a great impression on us only when it gives us something which, even with all the efforts of our intellect, we cannot understand completely.

—ARTHUR SCHOPENHAUER

Art has such an impact on people that many strange things can happen in their souls: mysteries become clearer; opaque things become evident; complicated things become simple; what is probable becomes necessary. A real artist always simplifies.

—After HENRI AMIEL

Remember that you cannot do anything wonderful driven by competition; you cannot do anything noble from pride.

—JOHN RUSKIN

There are two very clear indications of real science and real art: the first inner sign is that a scholar or an artist works not for profit, but for sacrifice, for his calling; the second, outer sign is that his works are understandable to all people. Real science studies and makes accessible that knowledge which people at that period of history think important, and real art transfers this truth from the domain of knowledge to the domain of feelings.

Creating art is not as elevated a thing as many people guess, but certainly it is a useful and kind thing to do, especially if it brings people together and arouses kind feelings in them.

July 3

A person is enslaved to the extent he believes that his life has only a physical beginning.

Nothing can be done without faith. Hesitation can kill a person, or it can destroy whole nations. Why is it so difficult to give liberation to people? Because when people do not have a deep faith they are not completely sure about their rights.

—F. ROBERT DE LAMENNAIS

They say that the highest good is freedom. And if freedom is goodness, then how can a free person be unhappy? If you see a person who is not happy you should know that he is not a free man; he is a slave of something. In order to be completely free, you should be ready to give to God all those things which you have received from him. You should be ready to unite your will with that of God.

—After EPICTETUS

When you have no freedom, then your life becomes the life of an animal.

—GIUSEPPE MAZZINI

Human dignity and freedom are our constant necessities. So, let us keep them with us, or let us die with dignity.

—MARCUS TULLIUS CICERO

If you feel that you are not free, look for the reason inside you.

July 4

Punishment is a notion that humankind gradually outgrows.

A person has done evil, so another person, or a group of people, in order to fight this evil, cannot think of anything better than to create another evil, which they call punishment.

Every punishment is based, not on logic or on the feeling of justice, but on the desire to wish evil on those who have done evil to you or to another person.

Capital punishment is a very clear proof that our society's organization is far from being a Christian one.

Everything about our present system of punishments and about all criminal law will be thought of by future generations in the same way that we think of cannibalism or human sacrifice to ancient pagan gods. "How did they not see the uselessness and cruelty of those things which they did?" our descendants will say about us.

To punish others is like putting more wood in the fire. Every crime already has punishment in itself, and it is more cruel and more just than the punishment created by people.

We should remember that the desire to punish is part of a very low animal feeling which should be suppressed, and which should not be a part of our reality.

July 5

Solomon and Job knew and spoke wisely about the uselessness of human life. The first was the happiest, the second the unhappiest of all men. One knew the vanity of pleasure; the other, the reality of misfortune.

—BLAISE PASCAL

Follow the best way of life you possibly can, and habit will make this way suitable and pleasant for you.

This is the divine law of life: that only virtue stands firm. All the rest is nothing.

—PYTHAGORAS

If you fear woes and misfortunes, then you are already unhappy. Those who fear misfortunes usually deserve them.

—CHINESE PROVERB

Happiness and calmness are neither inside us nor outside us. They are in God, who is both inside and outside us.

—BLAISE PASCAL

Everything is from God; therefore, everything is good. Evil is goodness which we did not understand because of our shortsightedness.

When one understands that kind of evil which is in his deeds, then all other misfortunes to which he can be subjected are nothing as compared with the pleasure and freedom he can then experience.

July 6

Neither the descriptions of war nor its terrible cruelties and atrocities can stop people from participating in it. One reason for this is that by viewing the atrocities of war, everyone comes to understand that if such a terrible thing can exist and be accepted by people, then there must be some reason for its existence.

A witness recounted his experience in the Russian-Japanese war, when he was on the upper deck of the *Variag* battleship during a Japanese attack. It was a terrible sight. Everywhere there was blood, pieces of flesh, bodies with heads torn away, the smell of blood so strong it made even the most tough and hardest men dizzy. The armored cannon tower suffered most of all. A shell exploded on top of it and killed a young officer who was the chief of the ship's artillery. Only one thing was left of the poor man; it was his fist, the hand which held the instrument. Two of four sailors who stood next to their commander were torn into pieces, and the other two had terrible injuries; afterwards both had their legs amputated, and then the remains of their legs were cut off again completely. The commander of the battleship had a small injury in his head, in the temples. Filth, terrible illnesses, hunger, fire, destruction, evil—this is military glory, this is war.

—HENRI HARDUIN GARDUEN

War is now more terrible than at any period in human history.

—GUY DE MAUPASSANT

The time has come to talk about the evils of war. It is not true that the existence of wars proves their necessity. The history of mankind says that such things should not happen.

July 7

To deny God is to deny yourself as a spiritual and intellectual being.

I know God and soul not by their definition, but in another way entirely. Striving to define God destroys this knowledge in me. I know that God exists, that my soul exists; this knowledge is clear to me because I was given it. I have not the slightest doubt about the existence of God, if I ask: What am I? Who am I? My legs are not me; my arms are not me; my head is not me; my feelings are not me; even my thought is not me. Then what am I? I am myself, I am my soul. No matter which side I approach this question, I inevitably come to God. The beginning of my life is God, the beginning of my existence is God. The same with the soul. If I want to know the truth, I know that at the beginning of all is my soul; if I want to understand my feeling of love and necessity for goodness, then I again find the source of this in my soul.

God exists. We should not prove this; to deny God is madness. God lives in my conscience, in the conscience of all humanity, in all our universe, and we talk to God in the most important moments of sadness or joy.

—GIUSEPPE MAZZINI

Life in this world goes according to somebody's will—someone performs special actions upon all life in this world, and touches all our lives. That which performs these actions is what we call God.

July 8

That feeling which solves all of the contradictions of human life and gives one the greatest bliss is known to all people: this feeling is love.

Pay bad people with your goodness; fight their hatred with your kindness. Even if you do not achieve victory over other people, you will conquer yourself.

—Henri Amiel

Love destroys death and makes it empty; it gives meaning to senseless things; from unhappiness, love makes real happiness.

Fire purifies everything in the material world; love purifies everything in the spiritual world.

—Henri Amiel

The less love a person has, the more he suffers.

If you are in a difficult situation, a low mood, if you are afraid of other people and of yourself, if you are tormented, then tell yourself: "I will love everyone whom I meet in this life." Try to follow this rule; and you will see that everything will find its way, and everything will seem simple, and you will no longer have doubts or fears.

July 9

People mistakenly think that virtue lies in the knowledge of many things. What is important is not the quantity but the quality of knowledge.

Socrates thought that stupidity was incompatible with wisdom, but he never said that ignorance was stupidity.

—XENOPHON

We live in the age of philosophy, science, and intellect. Huge libraries are open for everyone. Everywhere we have schools, colleges, and universities which give us the wisdom of the people from many previous millennia. And what then? Have we become wiser for all this? Do we better understand our life, or the meaning of our existence? Do we know what is good for our life?

—JEAN JACQUES ROUSSEAU

Reading too much is harmful to your independence of thought. The greatest thinkers I've met among scholars are people who do not read too much.

—GEORGE LICHTENBERG

Do not fear the lack of knowledge, fear false knowledge. All evil in this world comes from false knowledge.

Knowledge born in argument and discussion is to be doubted.

In the world today, real faith has in most cases been replaced by public opinion. People do not believe in God, but they believe in many minor things which are taught by other people.

People's misfortunes are caused not because they do not know their duties, but because they misunderstand their duties.

God gives a choice to every soul between truth and peace.
—RALPH WALDO EMERSON

Faith is not achieved by a majority of votes.

The major reason for the evil that exists today is the absence of faith in people of our time.

Truly virtuous is the person who gives his love to the weak.

Power is given to a person, not to oppress the weak, but to support and to help the weak.

—JOHN RUSKIN

Give to every man that asketh of thee; and of him that taketh away thy goods ask them not again. And as ye would that men should do to you, do ye also to them likewise.

—LUKE 6:30–31

Every kind thing is a virtue. To give water to a thirsty person, or to pick up a stone from a road, or to convince your neighbors and friends that they should be virtuous, or to show a traveler his way, or to smile looking into your neighbor's face—all this is virtue.

—MOHAMMED

If a rich person could be truly virtuous, then he would stop being rich very quickly.

July 12

The foundation of love is in each person's understanding of the unity of the divine spark which lives in all people.

All that brings unification to people is goodness and beauty; all that brings separation among them is evil. All people know this: it is firmly inscribed on our hearts.

Every good or charitable action, every unprofitable assistance which supports other people in need, when we come to its origins and foundations, becomes a mysterious and unexplainable thing, because it comes out of the mysterious understanding of the unity of all living beings, and it can be explained by nothing else.

—ARTHUR SCHOPENHAUER

We are separate beings, it seems, but in our inner life we are closely connected with all living things.

We can feel some of the vibrations of this spiritual world; some of them have not reached us yet, but they are moving, as the vibrations of light from the distant stars are moving across the universe; they move, though they are not yet visible to our eyes.

July 13

The existing order of things can be improved.

Wise consumption is much more complicated than wise production. What five people will produce, one person can very easily consume, and the question for each individual and for every nation is not how are we to produce, but how our products are to be consumed.

—JOHN RUSKIN

You can torture people; you can treat them as if they were animals; you can abuse them in all ways; you can kill them as if they were summer flies. But people will remain free in the highest sense because they have eternal souls.

—JOHN RUSKIN

In order to fulfill the law of God as we understand it, a joint effort must be made by many people. Then, maybe slowly, we will move to an understanding of this divine law.

God's kingdom is the fulfillment among mankind of God's will, according to the measure in which it is revealed to us.

In the life of the world, thousands of years look like one year. Therefore, we should work hard at the fulfillment of eternity, and we should wait for the day when religion will enlighten this world completely.

The kingdom of God on earth is the final purpose and desire of humankind.

—IMMANUEL KANT

In religious services we should understand, not the rituals, not unnatural things which can be performed only by a priest; in religion, we should understand love for God and for our neighbor.

—ALEXANDR ARKHANGELSKY

The kingdom of God is inside us; therefore look for the kingdom of God inside you and the rest will take care of itself, in the best possible way.

July 15

My material life is subject to suffering and death, and no effort of mine can release me from suffering or death. My spiritual life is subject neither to suffering nor death. Therefore, salvation from suffering and death lies in only one thing: in the transfer of my conscious "self" from the material to the spiritual.

The way to understand this world is to understand your inner self. With the help of love, and by virtue of the love of others, we understand other beings: people, animals, plants, stones, heavenly bodies; and we understand the attitudes of these beings to themselves; and these attitudes create the whole world as we know it. The way to understanding is based on love, on unification with all other creatures in the world.

Yet not My will, but Thine be done.

—LUKE 22:42

The essence of love of God is in the desire of the soul for its creator, for unity with this higher light.

—The TALMUD

This eternal beginning in you has always existed, it exists now, and it will always exist: its time will never end.

—THE BRAHMIN'S WISDOM

That which we understand as the happiness or unhappiness of our animal "self" depends on the highest spiritual will.

July 16

Nothing can support idleness better than empty chatter. People would be better to keep silent and not speak the boring, empty things they routinely say to entertain themselves. How can they endure it?

The person who speaks much will seldom fulfill all his words in his actions. A wise person is always wary lest his words surpass his actions.

—CHINESE WISDOM

First think, then speak. Stop when told "enough." A person is higher than an animal because of his ability to speak, but he is lower than an animal if he cannot properly use this ability.
—MUSLIH-UD-DIN SAADI

Those people speak most who do not have much to say.

If you want to stop a person from an action, ask him to speak more on the topic. The more people speak, the less desire they have to act.

—THOMAS CARLYLE

The less you speak, the more you will work.

July 17

The foundation of ancient societies was violence. The basis of our contemporary society is wise concord, the negation of violence.

Ye have heard that it hath been said, An eye for an eye, and a tooth for a tooth: But I say unto you, That ye resist not evil: but whosoever shall smite thee on thy right cheek, turn to him the other also.

—MATTHEW 5:38–39

He who is really skillful in communicating with people is usually a humble and quiet person. This is called the virtue of nonresistance. This is called harmony with Heaven.

—LAO-TZU

Some people think that it is impossible to rule other people without violence. And so they do to people as other people do with horses, when they blind their eyes so that they will more obediently walk in a circle.

For what purpose is a man's intellect if you are going to influence him only with violence?

In all cases, when people use violence, you should try to convince them not to. You should try to apply wise, convincing arguments, appealing not to the everyday world, but to their higher spiritual understanding. Then, when you succeed, you will have the complete satisfaction of your conscience.

July 18

People believe in eternal life because they believe that life's beginning is spiritual, and therefore eternal.

In our soul is the sign of eternity.

—William Ellery Channing

Our biggest desire is to live forever. But when we are freed from this body, we will not wish to come back. Is there such a child who, once born, would like to return to the womb of his mother? Is there a man who, freed from prison, would like to return to it? In the same way, a person should not be afraid about the future liberation from his body, if he is not connected too closely with this material life.

—Tables of the Babids, a Muslim sect from Persia

A person is not afraid to die only after he understands that he was never born, that he always existed, exists at present, and will always exist.

A person will believe in his eternity when he understands that his life is not a wave, a period of time, but the eternal movement which is manifested in this life only as a wave.

Those who believe that their life has not begun with their birth and will not end with death find it much easier to live a good life than those who do not understand or believe this.

July 19

Really true, good, and great things are always simple.

The language of truth is always simple.
>—Lucius Annaeus Seneca

Very often the simplest and least educated people can easily and unconsciously understand the meaning of life while the most scholarly people lack this ability, because they have been too educated to understand the simple things that are basic to all people.

The clearest and simplest notions are almost always concealed by sophisticated meditations.
>—Marcus Tullius Cicero

If you want to find an example to follow, you should look among simple, humble folk. There is real greatness only in those who do not advertise themselves, and who do not understand themselves as great.

July 20

The feeling of compassion for other living beings reminds me of the feeling of pain in our body. Just as you can become less sensitive to pain in your body with time, you can become less compassionate to others.

The first condition to bringing religion into your life is manifesting love and pity toward all living creatures.

—CHINESE WISDOM

Compassion for animals is closely connected with character type. You can say with confidence that he who is cruel to animals cannot be a kind man.

—ARTHUR SCHOPENHAUER

Every murder is terrible. But most terrible is the murder in which you want to eat the creature you have killed, when you kill for the satisfaction of your stomach.

—MIKHAIL GOLDSTEIN

When the suffering of another creature causes you to feel pain, do not submit to the initial desire to flee from the suffering one, but on the contrary, come closer, as close as you can to him who suffers, and try to help him.

Love is the manifestation of the divine nature which exists above time. Love is not only a way of life, it is an action directed toward the goodness of others.

There is no love in the future. Love can exist only in the present moment. A man who does not manifest love in the present does not love at all.

Be kind even if the world blames you. It is better than the converse when a person is praised by others but continues to be bad.

The New Testament reflects a very simple faith: faith in God and respect for Him. It is the same in following the law; there is only one law: love your neighbor.

—BENEDICTUS SPINOZA

Certainly, it is painful to recall all the things which you could have done in the past but did not: some charity, for example; a time you denied to those who expected help from you; or when you blocked the joyful understanding of completing an action you should have finished.

Faith is not true faith if love is not in harmony with it.

The door to heaven is opened to you to the same extent you want it. Get rid of your troubles and problems, and direct your soul to spiritual things. Be attentive, and fulfill your duty without thinking about the consequences. You should not guide events, but be guided by events.

—INDIAN WISDOM

What doth it profit, my brethren, though a man say he hath faith, and have not works? Can faith save him? If a brother or sister be naked, and destitute of daily food, and one of you say unto them, Depart in peace, be ye warmed and filled; notwithstanding ye give them not those things which are needful to the body; what doth it profit? Even so faith, if it hath not works, is dead, being alone. . . . Ye see then how that by works a man is justified, and not by faith only. . . . For as the body without the spirit is dead, so faith without works is dead also.

—JAMES 2:14–18, 24, 26

A person who knows the law but does not fulfill it reminds me of one who plows the land but does not put seed in it.

—EASTERN WISDOM

If a person is not in a hurry to fulfill the things which he understands as the law of God, then he believes neither in the law, nor in God.

July 23

Effort is the necessary condition of moral perfection.

Those who think that they can live a high spiritual life whose bodies are filled with idleness and luxuries are mistaken.

The body is the first student of the soul.

—HENRY DAVID THOREAU

Nothing more can be considered as real merit for a person than his effort. Only in his effort is a person shown in his real light.

—The KORAN

If you were abused, make an effort to love those who have abused you. If you have abused someone, make an effort to correct the evil which you created.

July 24

When one understands life's law, one manifests the part of God which lives inside him.

Every man, from the king to the poorest pauper, should seek his own perfection, because only self-perfection improves mankind.

—Confucius

In the long run, people achieve only that which they have set as goals for themselves; therefore, set the highest possible goals for yourself.

The fulfillment of the law of goodness has nothing in common with everyday material prosperity. Sometimes material prosperity and moral goodness clash in conflict. These sufferings lead to the highest elevation of spirit.

July 25

Sometimes we cannot see any connection between our suffering and our sin, but this connection definitely exists.

"I was repaid with evil for the goodness which I have done." But if you love those for whom you did good, then you have already received your reward. Therefore, all that you do with love, you do for yourself.

The reward for virtue is the understanding of the good deed.

—MARCUS TULLIUS CICERO

Look for the causes of the evil from which you suffer in yourself. Sometimes this evil is the direct consequence of your activity; sometimes it happens after a lengthy period of transformation of an evil which you committed long ago. But the source is always in you, and salvation from it lies in changes in your actions, your way of life.

July 26

In every faith, only what is spiritual is true.

God is a spirit, and those who worship Him must worship in spirit and truth.

—JOHN 4:24

If you do not believe that at its beginning, your life came from spirit, why are you looking for it elsewhere, thinking that you can find spirit in other places? He who behaves in this way is like the man who burns a lantern in bright sunlight.

Do not be afraid to get rid of things which distract your attention—everything material, everything which can be seen or can be felt. The more you purify the spiritual core of your faith, the firmer your faith will be.

July 27

Knowledge is a tool, not a purpose.

People know little, because they try to understand those things which are not open to them for understanding: God, eternity, spirit; or those which are not worth thinking about: how water becomes frozen, or a new theory of numbers, or how viruses can transmit illnesses. How to live your life is the only real knowledge.

People who think that the most important thing in life is knowledge remind me of a butterfly who flies into the flame of a candle, and in so doing burns, and extinguishes the light.

The title "scholar" suggests that a person has gone to school, and that he studied, but it does not mean that he has acquired any truly important knowledge.
—George Lichtenberg

The purpose of life is the fulfillment of the law of God, not the acquisition of ever more knowledge.

July 28

Repentance always precedes perfection. It is sad that people think repentance is unnecessary.

It is dangerous to see the cause of evil as lying outside ourselves; for them repentance becomes impossible.

—FREDERICK WILLIAM ROBERTSON

Not to accept your mistakes is to increase them.

I have a burden on my soul. During all my long life, I did not make anyone happy, neither my friends, nor my family, nor even myself. I have done many evil things. . . . I was the cause of the beginning of three big wars. About 800,000 people were killed because of me on the battlefields, and their mothers, brothers, and widows cried for them. And now this stands between me and God.

—OTTO VON BISMARCK

You should live in such a way that you can confide anything on your mind.

July 29

The more important something is in your life, the more harmful it can be for you in the future if you abuse it. The misfortunes and woes of people often come from the abuse of the most precious tool of our life: intellect.

God gave his spirit, his intellect, to us, so that we can understand his will and fulfill it; but we misuse it and apply this spirit for the fulfillment of our own will.

When the intellect becomes the slave of vices and passions, the supporter of lies, it becomes not only a perversion, but an illness, and we cannot see the difference between truth and falsehood, good and evil, virtue and vice.

—WILLIAM ELLERY CHANNING

When a person tries to apply his intellect to the question "Why do I exist in this world?" he becomes dizzy. The human intellect cannot find the answers to such questions. What does this mean? This means that our intellect is not given to us to find a solution for this question. Our intellect can only answer the question: "How shall I live?" And the answer is simple: "We should live so as to bring good to all people."

The purpose of the intellect is to reveal the truth; therefore it is a harmful misconception to pervert the truth with intellectual efforts.

July 30

Only those who know their weaknesses can be tolerant of the weaknesses of their neighbors.

My children, if someone abuses you with words, do not pay much attention; be quiet at your prayer, and ask your friends to settle the dispute and find peace between you and those who have abused you.

—The TALMUD

The man who cannot forgive destroys a bridge which he will have to cross, because every person needs forgiveness.

—EDWARD HERBERT

Almost always, when we look deep into our souls, we can find there the same sins which we blame in others. If we do not find a particular sin in our soul, then we should look more closely, and we will find even worse sins there.

A deep river is not troubled if you throw a stone into it. If a religious person is hurt by criticism, then he is not a river but a shallow pool. Forgive others, and then you will receive forgiveness.

—MUSLIH-UD-DIN SAADI

If we can put ourselves into the place of other people, we lessen our pride.

July 31

If Christians would follow the law, there would be no rich and no poor.

And, behold, one came and said unto him, Good Master, what good thing shall I do, that I may have eternal life? ... Jesus said unto him, if thou wilt be perfect, go and sell that thou hast, and give to the poor, and thou shalt have treasure in heaven: and come and follow me.
—MATTHEW 19:16, 21

A rich person can be insensitive and completely indifferent to the woes of others.
—The TALMUD

Wealth reminds me of manure in the field. When it is in a big pile it makes a bad smell. But when it is distributed everywhere across the field, it makes the soil fertile.

A person must completely close his eyes on his morals, that in a Christian society so filled with people in need, there are other people who are so proud to have great wealth.

The intellect can liberate a person; the less of an intellectual life one has, the less liberated one is.

If you wish to do no evil then there is not a single good deed which you cannot do.

—CHINESE WISDOM

A wise person lives in accordance with his desires, because he wants only that which is attainable. Such a person is free.

Diogenes said, "A wise man becomes free when he is ready to die at any moment." He wrote to the Persian king, "You cannot enslave truly free people, just as you cannot enslave a fish. You may capture them, but you cannot force them to serve; they prefer to die as captives. So, what would it profit you to imprison them?" This is a speech of a really free man, a man who recognizes his own freedom.

—EPICTETUS

We have created a way of life which is contrary to mankind's moral and physical nature, and yet we want to be free while living this kind of life.

Freedom cannot be achieved by looking for it, but in looking for truth. Freedom should not be a purpose, but a consequence.

Freedom cannot be granted to you by others. Each person can liberate only himelf.

August 2

If you are a material being, then death is the end of everything. But if you are a spiritual being, then the body limits your spiritual being, and death is only a change.

Our body limits the spiritual divine spark which we call our soul. In the way that a vessel gives form to the liquid or gas which is put into it, our body gives form to our spiritual being. If the vessel is broken, that which was in it no longer retains the form it had and flows out. Does it receive a new form? Is it united with other beings? We know nothing of this. After death the soul becomes something different, something indescribable.

Death is one step in a continuous development.
—THEODORE PARKER

Our last day does not bring destruction, only a change.
—MARCUS TULLIUS CICERO

Death is a liberation of the soul from the material personality in which it existed in this world.

For those who live a spiritual life, there is no death.

We expect rewards for goodness, and punishments for the bad things which we do. Often, they are not immediately forthcoming. Both evil and good exist in the life of the spirit, though, which is outside time, and though we may not see clear indications of reward or punishment, nevertheless, we feel reward or punishment with our conscience.

You should be in a hurry to do good works, even small ones, and to avoid sin. One good thing leads to another, and one sin causes another. The reward for virtue is virtue, and the punishment for vice is more vice.

—The TALMUD

The worst punishment is the understanding that you failed to properly use those good things which were given to you. Do not expect a big punishment. There can be no harder punishment than this remorse.

You seek the cause of evil, and it is only in yourself.
—JEAN JACQUES ROUSSEAU

Doing good is the only sure path to bliss.

Do not expect some tangible reward for your goodness; your actions are their own reward. In the same way, do not think that you can hope to avoid punishment of your evil acts, for your punishment already lies in your soul. You are mistaken if you think that the pain in your soul was caused by anything else.

August 4

Self-abnegation is not the rejection of your entire self, just the rejection of your animal being.

Every person has within himself the capability to understand the life of all humanity. This capability is hidden deep in the soul, but it exists, and sooner or later, a person will find it.

—EDWARD CARPENTER

The greatest bliss a person can know is the state of complete freedom and happiness that can come only through self-sacrifice and love.

Deny your personality, and you will come to understand the highest good in life: love.

Real life starts with self-sacrifice.

—THOMAS CARLYLE

The more a person gives to other people, and the less he asks for himself, the better for him. The less he gives to others, and the more he wants for himself, the worse for him. Our contemporaries think it the reverse.

August 5

For the most part, false and harmful opinions are distributed and supported by influence. We are too likely to accept the views and thoughts of other people without trying to investigate them deeper and further ourselves. Unimportant people are those who accept other people's thoughts without developing them themselves.

Your thought is easily influenced by the presence of another soul; a person can be completely free only when he is alone.

Nothing is more harmful than a bad example set by others. They bring into our life notions which never would have occurred to us without an example.

Do not allow yourself to be infected by the mood or spirit of those who abuse you; do not step onto their path.
—MARCUS AURELIUS

A person can easily grow accustomed to living a lie, especially if he sees everyone around him living in the same way.

False ideas which gain currency can easily be recognized by the loud fanfare with which they are accompanied. Real truth does not need any outer embellishments.

The possibility of influencing others causes a person with high morals to be more strict about his words and actions which could influence other people.

August 6

The intellect is the only fit guide for human life.

The light of the body is the eye: therefore when thine eye is single, thy whole body also is full of light; but when thine eye is evil, thy body also is full of darkness. Take heed therefore that the light which is in thee be not darkness.

—LUKE 11:34–35

A man who lives an intellectual life is like a man who carries a lantern in front of him to light his way. Such a person will never come to a dark place, because the light of his intellect moves before him. There is no fear of death in this kind of life, because the lantern which moves before you lights your way to your last minute, and you follow it to the end as calmly and quietly as you have all of your life.

Some people live and act according to their own thoughts, and some according to the thoughts of others; this is a crucial distinction between people.

August 7

Vanity has no limits.

A person filled with vanity is so involved with himself that there is no room inside him for anyone or anything else.

—Pan

As rules go, "You should behave just as other people behave" is among the most dangerous; it almost always results in your behaving badly.

—Jean de La Bruyère

You could choose no worse way to guide your life than to follow the opinions of other people.

When we praise other people it is because we think that they look like us; often to respect a person means to put him on the same level as oneself.

—Jean de La Bruyère

Real virtue never looks back on its shadow, fame.

—Johann Wolfgang von Goethe

It's not wise to be interested in fame and the appreciation of others, because no two people's opinions about what is good are the same.

The opinion of a revered writer or thinker can have a deep influence on society; it can also be a big obstacle to understanding real truth.

Divine truth may be revealed in the speech of children, or in the ravings and nightmares of madmen; or in the ordinary conversations of simple people. And weak and false thoughts may be found in books which have come to be considered great, or even sacred.

Many statements which are accepted as truth because they have been passed down to us by tradition look like truth only because we have never tested them, never thought about them in a more precise way.

For the majority of mankind, religion is a habit, or, more precisely, tradition is their religion. Though it seems strange, I think that the first step to moral perfection is your liberation from the religion in which you were raised. Not a single person has come to perfection except by following this way.

—HENRY DAVID THOREAU

A thought which is expressed in the Old Testament, or in the New Testament, or in the Koran or in the Indian divine book the Upanishads, does not become a truth because it is expressed in a book which is considered to be holy. If we think that every word in every holy book is true, then we have created an idol.

Any important thought, no matter where it comes from, should be discussed; and every thought, no matter who said it, should be given attention.

August 9

The majority of evils people commit are the result, not of an evil will, but of the dissemination of evil thoughts which people accept and follow uncritically.

Material results are the manifestations of unseen forces: an artillery shell that comes to us was shot from an unseen cannon at an unknown time. In the same way, all important events originate in a thought.

—HENRI AMIEL

Our actions are neither as good nor as vicious as our desires.

—LUC DE VAUVENARGUES

Think only good thoughts, and with time they will become good deeds.

Thoughts which create evil actions are much worse than the acts themselves. You can stop doing a bad thing, and repent, and not repeat it. But bad thoughts are repeated again and again, and cause other bad actions; bad thoughts follow one after another.

Think good thoughts, and your thoughts will be turned into good actions. Everything begins in thought. Guiding your thoughts is one of the keys to self-perfection. If you suffer misfortunes in your life, look for their cause, not in your actions, but in the thoughts which inspired them, and try to improve those thoughts. If you are inspired by an event in your life, look for its origins in your previous thoughts which caused the event.

You make your decisions in the present, and the present exists out of time; it is a tiny moment where two periods—the past and the future—meet. In the present you are always free to make your choice.

A wise man was asked what was the most important time, person, and thing in life. He answered, "The most important time is the present time, because at this time a person has power over himself. The most important person is the one with whom you deal at present, because there is no guarantee that you will ever be able to deal with any other person in this world. The most important thing is to love this person, because everyone is sent into this world with the sole purpose of loving other people."

Only when we use every minute of our life will we know that we are eternal.

—HARRIET MARTINEAU

A most dangerous temptation is the temptation to prepare to live, instead of living. The future does not belong to you. Therefore, remember to live the best way you know *now*. The only perfection necessary is perfection in love, which can be reached only in the present. It's why we came into this world.

The present is the moment in which the divine nature of life is revealed. Let us respect our present time; God exists in this time.

August 11

A person dies as he lives his spiritual life, alone.

What you do, you possess. You must believe that eternal goodness exists that is within you, and that it grows and develops as long as you live.

—Ralph Waldo Emerson

You alone plan to commit a sin, you alone plan to do evil; and you alone can escape sin and purify your thoughts. Only your inner self can damn you, and only your inner self can save you.

—Dhammapada, a book of Buddhist wisdom

A person may ask God or other people for help, but only his good life can help him, and this he must do on his own.

Every person has a depth to his inner life, an essence that cannot be explained. Sometimes you want to explain this essence to people, but you will see that it isn't possible to explain it to another person so that he understands.

Hence the need for your own channel of communication with God. Establish this channel and do not seek anything else.

The burden, the cross, which every man has to carry exists on two planes: a longer vertical plane, which is the will of God; and a much shorter, horizontal plane, which is a man's own will. If you orient your will so that it parallels the direction of God's will, then you will have no cross to carry, no burden.

Real happiness can be built only by harmonizing your life with the will of God.

—LUCY MALORY

He who is not with Me is against Me; and he who does not gather with Me, scatters.

—LUKE 11:23

If you want to fulfill the will of God, all will be good; if you want to fulfill your own will, and it does not coincide with the will of God, all will be evil.

The only way to know God and to believe in eternity is to unite your own will with the will of God.

To be wise, you must follow your intellect, even though such a way of life is often attacked.

The heavens do not approve when we sin, and the earth does not approve when we are virtuous.

—The TALMUD

Do not be interested in the quantity of people who respect and admire you, but in their quality. If bad people dislike you, so much the better.

—LUCIUS ANNAEUS SENECA

Human intellect is a divine lamp, and its light penetrates to the depth of things.

—EASTERN WISDOM

You should not be upset by the sight of wisdom being criticized. Wisdom would not be real wisdom if it did not reveal the stupidity of a bad life, and people would not be people if they endured this revelation without criticism.

August 14

People have become too accustomed to the use of force. Life without violence seems impossible for them to imagine.

Two ways exist to guide human activity. One is to force a person to act against his wishes; the other is to guide a person's wishes, to persuade him with reasoning. One is the way of violence: it is used by ignorant people, and it leads to complete disappointment. The other is supported by experience, and is always successful.

—ABRAHAM COMB

Without faith in God, you can force people to act, but you cannot convince them. You can become a tyrant, but not a teacher.

—GIUSEPPE MAZZINI

People are wise beings; they possess the ability to live according to the dictates of their intellect, and sooner or later, they will evolve from a state of violence to a state of complete harmony and understanding. And every act of violence makes this time more distant from today.

All other arguments against meat eating, no matter how strong they are, are meaningless in relation to the fact that animals have the same life spirit that exists in us. We should feel that by taking an animal life we commit something close to suicide. No other argument against meat eating is necessary for those who have this inner feeling.

Eating a lot of meat can make your body stronger, but it weakens your mind.

—PLUTARCH

It is very important not to kill children's natural taste by forcing them to become meat eaters, not only for their health, but for the sake of their character. We do not know the reason, but we know that people who eat a lot of meat are usually cruel.

—JEAN JACQUES ROUSSEAU

We cannot close our eyes to those people who eat meat for the satisfaction of their pampered tastes.

The logical arguments against meat eating are not strong enough. Logic is good, but in some cases it falls short. But know this: the more compassion a person shows other living creatures, the kinder and better he is. To kill animals, whether for sport or for fuel, is very cruel.

August 16

We are spiritually connected on all sides, not only with people but with all living creatures.

Someone told me once that every person has an element of good and an element of bad within him, and that either the good or the bad can be manifested according to the person's mood. We possess within us two different ways of understanding this world. One is the feeling of being divided, distanced, and alienated from each other; in this state, all things seem gloomy to us. We feel nothing except jealousy, indifference, and hatred. I would like to call the opposite way of understanding the understanding of universal unification. In this state, all people seem very close to us, and all are equal among themselves. This state, therefore, arouses compassion and love in us.

—Arthur Schopenhauer

All people have the same origin, are bound by the same law, and were created for the same purpose.

Therefore, we should have one faith, one purpose to our actions, one banner under which we live and fight.

—Giuseppe Mazzini

We should always try to find those things which do not separate us from other people but which unite us. To work against each other, to be angry and turn your back on each other, is to work against nature.

—Marcus Aurelius

Try to understand the unity of all living things. Try to serve and suffer with all living beings.

Kindness is a necessary addition to everything.

All the best qualities of mankind are meaningless and worthless without kindness, and even the worst vices can be easily forgiven with kindness.

There is a natural kindness which comes from our external attributes, from our inheritance, audience, good or bad indigestion, success, etc. This kind of kindness is very pleasant, both for the person who experiences it and for the people around him. And there is another type of kindness which comes from inner, spiritual work. This kindness is less attractive, but although the first kindness can easily change or be transformed into hatred, the second kind of kindness will never disappear and will constantly grow.

The goodness which you do gives you pleasure, but not satisfaction. No matter how much goodness you do, you should wish to do more and more.

—CONFUCIUS

Kindness is the major quality of the soul. If a person is not kind, it is because he was subjected to some lie, passion, or temptation which violated his natural state.

August 18

Christianity is true because it can answer the most distant, abstract questions, and at the same time, it can solve all practical issues of life as well. It established the kingdom of God in the spiritual life of every individual, and in the spiritual life of humanity in general.

Christ was sent to this world to bring good news. This was his major work. But do they teach this thing in his name? He wanted to change slavery into freedom. Is this taught in his name? Were they fulfilled, the things which he wanted to fulfill? Did poor people hear the good news? Have the broken hearts been cured? Can the blind people see? Have all the shackles been taken from the prisoners? Are the inmates set free? No. Christ is still on his cross, waiting for his apostles. They should come as soon as possible, because the suffering is terrible, and his eyes are tired of looking to the east and waiting for the sunrise of the time of the lord.

—F. ROBERT DE LAMENNAIS

Religion is true not because it was taught by the saints, but the saints taught it because it is true.

—GOTTHOLD EPHRAIM LESSING

Only religion destroys egoism and selfishness, so that one starts to live life not only for himself. Only religion destroys the fear of death, only religion gives us the meaning of life, only religion creates equality among people, only religion sets a person free from outer pressures. We must believe those spiritual doctrines which provide a very simple and practical guide for every one of us.

August 19

Life is constant movement, and therefore goodness in life is not a certain state, but the direction of movement. This direction is not in serving yourself, but God.

Some people seek goodness in power, others find it in science, others in dissipation. Those people who are really close to goodness understand that real goodness for one is when all people have this goodness and share it among themselves.

—BLAISE PASCAL

Happiness is a thing which a person wishes only for himself; goodness is a thing which a person wishes for himself and for others. Happiness can be achieved by struggle; goodness, on the contrary, by being humble.

Real goodness is to serve God.

You should do goodness without choosing to whom. Good things, once done, will never disappear, even if you forget about them. There is only one way to be happy, and this is a sure way: to do goodness and to share this goodness with others.

August 20

Anyone who is engaged in really important things is very simple because he does not have time to create unnecessary things.

Every desire abates, and every vice grows after it is satisfied.
—HENRI AMIEL

Every new desire is the beginning of a new wish, the beginning of a new sadness.
—VOLTAIRE

Pleasure, luxury—these things you call happiness, but I think that to wish nothing is the happiness of God, and when you wish to have only small things, then you make yourself closer to this divine and high happiness.
—SOCRATES

Nature requires small things; the existing law requires many excessive things.
—LUCIUS ANNAEUS SENECA

People can live without need and without jealousy only when they lead a life of moderation.

A fruitful prayer is the establishment in your conscious mind of the understanding of life's meaning, and you can experience this state during the best minutes of your life.

Prayer is understood as an inner formal religious service, a service to ask and achieve some compassion for yourself from the higher force; this is a misconception. On the other hand, the desire of our heart to please God with all our actions—this is the spirit of real prayer which should always exist in us.

—IMMANUEL KANT

But when ye pray, use not vain repetitions, as the heathen do: for they think that they shall be heard for their much speaking. Be not ye therefore like unto them: for your Father knoweth what things ye have need of, before ye ask him. After this manner therefore pray ye: Our Father which art in heaven, Hallowed be thy name. . . .

—MATTHEW 6:7–9

One hour of honest, serious thinking is more precious than weeks spent in empty talks.

You should pray every hour. The most necessary and the most difficult form of prayer is to remember—in spite of the numerous distractions of life—your obligations to God, to his law. You become scared, you become upset, you become embarrassed, you become too involved or distracted by something. But you should always remember who you are and what you should do. This is what a real prayer should be about. This is difficult in the beginning, but with time you can work and create this habit.

It is dangerous to disseminate the idea that our life is purely the product of material forces and that it depends entirely on these forces.

There are no people who can more confuse the notions of good and evil than the scholars of our time. Their science makes good progress in the study of the material world, but in the inner, spiritual life of humanity, it becomes an unnecessary and sometimes harmful thing.

False science and false religion express their dogmas in highly elevated language to make simple people think that they are mysterious, important, and attractive. But this mysterious language is not a sign of wisdom. The wiser a person is, the simpler the language he uses to express his thoughts.

—LUCY MALORY

The teaching about your inner life is the most useful one.

In our time science has started to give diplomas for idleness.

The real purpose of science is the understanding of the truth of this life. Its false purpose is the justification of evil in this world. These are the judicial sciences, political sciences, and especially theology, the science of religion.

If people were completely virtuous, they would never step aside from the truth.

And this is the condemnation, that light is come into the world, and men loved darkness rather than light, because their deeds were evil. For every one that doeth evil hateth the light, neither cometh to the light, lest his deeds should be reproved. But he that doeth truth cometh to the light, that his deeds may be made manifest, that they are wrought in God.

—John 3:19–21

Don't be afraid of a person in any position, in low or high standing, whether he is a scholar or an ignorant person. If you respect all people, you should love all people, and fear no one.

—William Ellery Channing

The consequences of any good thing which you have done in your life will die as soon as you step aside from the truth. The high spirit which lives in you and which is united with you is looking all the time for good and evil.

—Manu

Truth can be understood only by waiting and watching, and when you get one truth, two more will appear before you.

—John Ruskin

The truth is harmful only to evildoers. Those who do good love the truth.

People move, inconspicuously but ceaselessly, toward the kingdom of God, which will be achieved by unification in love.

Every single individual person, as well as all mankind together, will change, and will go on to higher stages without stopping in their development, the limit of which is God himself. And this time is coming.

—F. ROBERT DE LAMENNAIS

No, the word of all-powerful God has not been told completely. And his thought has not been understood completely in all its depth. He created and he creates, and he will create, for many eternal centuries after us; this the human mind cannot embrace.

—GIUSEPPE MAZZINI

I am come to send fire on the earth; and what will I, if it be already kindled? Suppose ye that I am come to give peace on earth? I tell you, Nay; but rather division.

—LUKE 12:49, 51

The constant struggle between flesh and spirit will never be finished. This struggle is eternal and the essence of life. The purpose of life is loving, the penetration of everything with love. It is the slow and gradual change from evil to good, it is the creation of the real life, the life filled with love.

The human world is always on the way to perfection, and the understanding of this process of perfection is one of mankind's biggest joys, and this joy is accessible to every person.

Work is the condition of existence in the material, physical world. If Robinson had not worked, he would have frozen to death and died from hunger, and everybody can see this. So labor is the necessary condition for the spiritual life as well, but not all people can see this clearly, though it is as obvious as the necessity of physical labor for the body.

If any would not work, neither should he eat.

—II Thessalonians 3:10

If you are doing nothing, it means you are doing bad things.

Those who do nothing, do bad things. Those who do nothing, have many associates and supporters. The brain of a lazy and idle person is the favorite stopping place of the devil.

Nature does not stop in its development, and it executes all kinds of idleness.

—Johann Wolfgang von Goethe

You should never be ashamed of any work, even the lowest and dirtiest, but you should be ashamed only of the dirtiest moral state, that is the idleness of your body, which is the necessary result of the consumption of the labor of others.

August 26

Justice is achieved not in striving for justice, but with love.

In order to hit the mark, you should aim farther than it stands, so you will achieve it; in order to be just, you should make a self-sacrifice, be unjust to yourself.

Not a single person can be completely just in all his deeds, but a just person can be completely different from an unjust one with his efforts, in the same way as a truthful man is different from a liar, with his efforts to speak only truth.

There is only one law of life which is really precious: though you meet all the time with injustice, remain humble.

—MARCUS AURELIUS

You cannot be completely just. One time you do too little, the other time you do too much. There is only one way not to sin against justice; always to change things, to improve things, to make them better.

The best and the most important object for every person is his inner self, his spiritual being.

A person who knows all sciences but does not know himself is a poor and ignorant person. He who does not know anything except for his inner spiritual self is an enlightened person.

When you feel the desire for power, you should stay in solitude for some time.

—HENRY DAVID THOREAU

The way to fame goes through the palaces, the way to happiness goes through the markets, the way to virtue goes through the deserts.

—CHINESE PROVERB

A person always has a place to be safe from all of his misfortunes, and this place is his soul.

If you could only know who you are, all your troubles would seem utterly unnecessary and trivial.

Faith is the foundation on which all else rests; it is the root of all knowledge.

There are two types of faith in this world. The first is faith in things other people say, faith in people; there are many varieties of this type of faith. The second is faith in God; this type of faith is unvarying, and it is necessary for all people.

Faith is the necessary property of the soul. Feel the essential meaninglessness of those things which are well-known to you, and the greatness of things which are unknown but important.

Cleave to the teachings of Christ completely, and let go of other teachings, just as a sailor reads his compass, though other signs around him might contradict it.

People who believe they do not have faith are wrong; they simply don't realize it, or don't want it, or cannot express it.

August 29

If, in his soul, a person understands God, he understands his connection to all the world's people.

Do not be proud, no matter what high position you occupy in life. In you and in me and in every other person lives the same God, the same life force; you look down on me in vain; we are all equal beings.

—INDIAN WISDOM

I am filled with a great thought: that of the greatness of my soul, its unity with God. My soul is not united with God in submission, but through its ability to understand Him, and through Him, to be eternal.

—HENRI AMIEL

We are all children of the same father, and it is unnatural not to love our brothers.

August 30

Those who are on top of the mountain can see the sunrise sooner than those who live in the valley. So, too, with those who achieve spiritual heights: they can see the heavenly sunrise sooner than those who live a material life. But the time will come when the sun will rise so high in the sky that everyone will see it.

We should hope that the day will come when all people perceive that the life of a man is great only in its service to his brothers, for he is united with them by God.

—EDWARD BROWN

Powerful forces are at work in this world. No one can stop them. We see their signs in a new understanding of religion, a new respect for people, a new feeling of brotherhood.

—WILLIAM ELLERY CHANNING

As soon as the higher ideal is put before us, all false ideals will fade away as the stars fade away when they meet the sun.

Any work of false art praised by critics is a door through which "hypocrites of art" enter our minds.

The creation and sale of most art today is pure prostitution. The comparison is true in every detail. Real art can only rarely be created even by a real artist; like a child in a mother's womb, it is the ripened fruit of his prior life. False art, though, can be ceaselessly produced by craftsmen, according to the dictates of a market. Like a faithful wife who loves her husband, real art does not need any excess decoration; like a prostitute, false art demands to be decorated. True art comes out of an artist's urgent need to express the feelings that have formed inside him, just as a mother needs to give birth to her baby. False art answers only to profit. Real art brings new feelings into our life, as a woman brings a new person into the world. False art corrupts: it makes a person dissipated, distracts him, weakens his spiritual power. Everyone must understand this, in order that they shun the terrible proliferation of this dirty, dissipated type of art which is, on its face, prostitution.

You cannot sell your talent, your genius; as soon as you do, you are a prostitute. You can sell your work, but not your soul.

—John Ruskin

Until they throw the money changers out of the temple of art, it will never be a real temple. But the time will come when these salesmen will be sent away from the temple of art.

September 1

Soldiers who stand idle in a shelter during a battle as reinforcements will try to involve themselves in almost any activity in order to distract themselves from the impending danger. It seems to me that people who want to save themselves from life behave like these soldiers: some distract themselves with vanity, some with cards, politics, laws, women, gambling, horses, hunting, wine, or state affairs.

It is difficult to imagine what wonderful changes would occur to human lives if people would stop poisoning themselves with brandy, wine, tobacco, and drugs.

They say that there is one religious sect that at the end of their gatherings they turn down the lights and have an orgy. In our society, people who participate in constant dissipations turn down the light of the intellect with addictive things such as drugs, alcohol, and tobacco.

Making yourself addicted is not a crime, but it is a preparation for crime.

Some people say, "It is not important if you drink or smoke." If it is of no importance, then why not just stop, if you know that you harm yourself and, with your example, others?

September 2

The closer people are to the truth, the more tolerant they are of the mistakes of others.

Those who don't believe in the spiritual foundations of their faith, who only pay lip service to the outer shell of their religious rituals, cannot be tolerant of others.

There is one hard and fast rule we must always remember: if a good end can be achieved only through bad means, either it is not good after all, or its time has not yet come.

Intolerant and power-hungry priests and pastors bring about the negation of religion.

—WILLIAM WARBURTON

Unbelievers can be equally intolerant as those who believe with crude, primitive understanding.

—JEAN FRANCE DUCLOS

A real truth, a real faith, needs neither worldly support nor an outer glamour, nor does it need to be forcefully introduced to others. God has time; for Him thousands of years pass as one. Those who feel the need to spread their faith through violence and force either lack faith in God, or in themselves.

God cannot be understood by the human intellect, only felt by the human heart. We only know that he exists, and regardless of whether we want it or not, we know this for sure.

The intellect is like a light that comes through a translucent glass: I see it, and though I do not know where it comes from, I know that it exists. We can say the same about God.

Believe in God, serve Him, but don't try to understand His essence. You will get nothing from your painful efforts except disappointment and fatigue. Do not even strive to find out whether he exists or not, just serve him as if he does, as if he is present everywhere. Nothing else is necessary.

—PHILEMON

No one except God comprehends the secret of the great beginning; no one can step outside himself.

—OMAR KHAYYAM

We can understand the existence of God with our intellect only when we understand our complete dependence on him, as if we have the same feeling an infant understands when his mother holds him. A baby does not know who feeds him, who warms him, who takes care of him, but he understands that there *is* someone who does this, and even he loves the force in whose power he rests.

Do not be alarmed if the notion of God is not clearly expressed to you. The more clearly it is expressed, the further it is from the truth, from its foundation.

Real goodness is not something that can be acquired in an instant, but only through constant effort, because real goodness lies in constantly striving for perfection.

The following words were carved on the bathroom of the king Jinx-Hang: "Renew yourself completely every day, and starting afresh, from the beginning."

—CHINESE WISDOM

The journey of the wise to virtue is as a journey to a remote land, or the ascent of a high mountain. People who travel to a faraway place start with a single step, and those who climb a high mountain start from the bottom.

—CONFUCIUS

And Jesus said unto him, No man, having put his hand to the plow, and looking back, is fit for the kingdom of God.

—LUKE 9:62

Strive for goodness without any expectations for rapid or noticeable success. You will not see the results of your efforts, because the further you progress, the higher the ideal of perfection toward which you strive rises. The effort of striving for goodness, the process itself, justifies our lives.

You should teach others with a good example, but if you teach with evil, then you do not teach, but destroy.

Then came Peter to him, and said, Lord, how oft shall my brother sin against me, and I forgive him? till seven times? Jesus saith unto him, I say not unto thee, Until seven times: but, Until seventy times seven.

—MATTHEW 18:21–22

Sinful people had once accepted their right to punish others—and most of our misfortunes started from this.

If you think someone is guilty of wronging you, forgive him. If you have never forgiven the guilty before, you will experience a new joy: the joy of forgiving.

Punishment is always cruel, always painful.

The American Indians had no laws, no punishments, and no government. They obeyed the moral understanding of good and evil that is part of every human nature.

—THOMAS JEFFERSON

The strongest proof that in the name of "science" we pursue unworthy and sometimes even harmful things is the existence of a science of punishment, which in itself is one of the most ignorant and offensive types of action known to man, a vestige of the lowest level of human development, lower than that of a child or a madman.

September 6

People jump back and forth in pursuit of pleasures only because they see the emptiness of their lives more clearly than they do the emptiness of whichever new entertainment attracts them.

—BLAISE PASCAL

The things we do to make our life more comfortable remind me of an ostrich who hides his head in order not to see his enemies. We behave even worse than an ostrich. In order to achieve some dubious questionable future, we definitely destroy our life in the clearly defined present time.

People today foolishly try to believe that all the world's senselessness and cruelty—the richness of the few, the great poverty of the many, the violence and warfare—happens outside their own lives and does not interfere with them and their way of life.

A misconception remains a misconception, even when it is shared by the majority of the people.

September 7

If life is good, then death which is the necessary part of life, is good as well.

Real life exists only in the present. The future has no meaning.

The purpose of real life is to fulfill the law of God, which exists eternally: it always existed, it exists now, and it always will exist.

Do not bother about what will happen someday, somewhere, in the far away distance, in a future time; think and be very attentive to what happens now, here, in this place.

—JOHN RUSKIN

As soon as you go into the future or the past, you go away from God, and you feel lonely, deserted, and enslaved.

The future does not really exist. It is created by us in the present.

There is a condition in which a person feels himself the architect of his life. It occurs when he concentrates all his efforts and all his intellect on the present moment.

September 8

At that time Jesus answered and said, I thank thee, O Father, Lord of heaven and earth, because thou hast hid these things from the wise and prudent, and hast revealed them unto babes. Even so, Father: for so it seemed good in thy sight.

—MATTHEW 11:25–26

The world would be a terrible place without newborn children, who bring with them innocence, and the hope of man's further perfection.

—JOHN RUSKIN

Childhood is blessed by heaven because it brings a piece of paradise into the cruelties of life. All these thousands of everyday births are fresh additions of innocence and purity, which fight against the end of mankind, and against our spoiled nature, and against our complete immersion into sin.

—HENRI AMIEL

O Lord our Lord, how excellent is thy name in all the earth! who hast set thy glory above the heavens. Out of the mouth of babes and sucklings hast thou ordained strength because of thine enemies, that thou mightest still the enemy and the avenger.

—PSALMS 8:1–2

What time could be better than childhood, and what virtues could be better than innocent joyfulness, and the need for love? They are the purest manifestations of life. You should respect every person, but you should respect a child above all, and not destroy the innocent purity of his soul.

September 9

The knowledge we now accept as science interferes with more than it supports the goodness of human life.

Astronomy, mechanics, physics, chemistry, and all other sciences together and differently, all study the particular sides of life, but they do not come to any conclusion about the spiritual life of mankind.

Science fulfills its purpose, not when it explains the reasons for the dark spots on the sun, but when it understands and explains the laws of our own life, and the consequences of violating these laws.

—JOHN RUSKIN

No matter how great our knowledge may be, it cannot help us fulfill our life's major purpose—our moral perfection.

The voice of conscience makes no mistakes. It wants, not the fulfillment of the animal self, but its denial or sacrifice.

A Christian who does not know where he goes (John 3:8), or what is given to him by God (John 3:34), does not know his life's real purpose.

—FYODOR STRAKHOV

As our self-interest diminishes, our anxieties disappear, and then comes quiet and firm joy, which always diffuses us with a good spiritual disposition and a clear conscience. Every good deed helps to kindle this feeling of joy within us. The egoist feels lonely, surrounded by threatening and alien events; all his desires are sunk in his own concerns. A kind person lives in a world of beneficent events, whose goodness matches his own.

—ARTHUR SCHOPENHAUER

A person who lives only for the concerns of his body may become lost in the labyrinth of an animal and sensual life, while the soul will always find truth; it will find the way.

—LUCY MALORY

The voice of your conscience can always be singled out above the noise of your other wishes, because it always wants something seemingly useless, seemingly senseless, seemingly incomprehensible, but at the same time something actually beautiful and good, which can be achieved only through effort.

September 11

The real faith attracts people to itself not because it promises goodness to those who believe, but because it is the only escape, not only from all the problems and troubles and misfortunes of our life, but also from the fear of death.

If you know that you lack faith, know also that you are in one of the most dangerous situations in this world a person can be in.

It is bad not to have something for which you are ready to die.

Look at the causes of the misfortunes from which mankind suffers. Push beyond the obvious causes to the root causes, and you will inevitably find that the most basic, the most important cause of each and every one of humanity's problems is the weakness of faith that comes from a false attitude to the world and its origin.

Salvation lies not in rituals and not in a particular creed, but in a clear understanding of the meaning of your life.

You cannot serve both god and the devil. Merely tending to the growth of your wealth has nothing to do with the requirements of the truly spiritual life.

It seems to me that the old prejudice that wealth brings happiness has begun to be discredited.

The love of great wealth commends you, "Bring me your soul as a sacrifice," and people will do so.

—Saint John Chrysostom

Excessive dress prevents the body from moving freely. Excessive wealth interferes with the movements of our soul.

—Demosthenes

The desire for wealth can never be satisfied. Those who have it are excited by the wish to have more, and yet more.

—Marcus Tullius Cicero

Do not fear poverty, but beware wealth.

If only people who seek wealth could clearly see what they would lose by having it, they would put the same amount of effort into getting rid of this wealth as they now put into acquiring it.

September 13

A wise man does not wish to change his situation, because he knows that it is possible to fulfill the law of God, the law of love, in every situation.

A wise man looks for everything inside of himself; a madman seeks for everything in others.

—CONFUCIUS

I never complain about my fate. Once, I did not have shoes, and I complained to God. I went into church with a heavy heart and in the church I saw a man without both feet. So I thanked God that he had given me both feet, and that my only problem was that they were unshod.

—MUSLIH-UD-DIN SAADI

A wise man innately knows how to act without searching, because he has the divine within himself. The further you search and seek, the less you know.

—LAO-TZU

You should treat your thoughts the way you treat your self, and treat your wishes the way you treat your children.

—CHINESE WISDOM

Try to establish an inner silence in yourself, a complete silence of your lips and your heart. Then you will hear how God speaks to us, and you will know how to fulfill His will.

The more upset a person is with other people, and with circumstances, and the more satisfied he is with himself, the further he is from wisdom.

September 14

Violence is harmful because it is usually dressed in wealth, and it therefore arouses some respect for those things which should arouse disgust.

People who have power are sure that it is only violence that guides people, and so they use violence to support the existing order. But the existing order is not based on violence, but on public opinion.

A person is not created either to subdue others, or to follow the orders of others. People are corrupted by both ways of behavior. In the first they assume too much importance, in the second, too little respect. In both ways there is very little dignity.

—Victor Considérant

Our life would become wonderful if we could see all the disgusting things which exist in it.

—Henry David Thoreau

Subduing people through violence is never justice.

—Blaise Pascal

He who depends on violence behaves wrongly. The maker of beautiful speeches is not wise, only he who is free from hatred and fear is truly wise.

—Buddhist wisdom

All violence is contrary to love: do not participate in violence.

September 15

The biggest obstacles to understanding the truth are lies disguised as truth.

In real life illusions can only transform our life for a moment, but in the domain of thoughts and the intellect, misconceptions may be accepted as truth for thousands of years, and make a laughingstock of whole nations, mute the noble wishes of mankind, make slaves from people and lie to them. These misconceptions are the enemies with which the wisest men in the history of mankind try to struggle. The force of the truth is great, but its victory is difficult. However, once you receive this victory, it can never be taken from you.

—ARTHUR SCHOPENHAUER

The exposure of a lie is as valuable to a community as a clearly expressed truth.

Freeing a person from misconceptions, false truths, and lies does not take anything from him; it gives him something important.

—ARTHUR SCHOPENHAUER

The progress of mankind is in revealing obstacles which are hiding from us.

September 16

Doubts do not destroy truth; they strengthen it.

Disbelief is not when a person believes or does not believe in something. It is when he prophesies those things in which he does not believe.

—HARRIET MARTINEAU

You will have moments in which you no longer believe in the existence of the spiritual dimension of life. Look at these moments as events in the development of your faith. A person who understands the spiritual nature of life may still at some point become afraid of death, usually for a short period of time, in the same way that you can see as you watch a scene at the theater and forget that you are watching a play, and become scared by what you are seeing as if it were real.

So it is in real life: in moments of self-delusion, a religious person forgets that what happens in his physical life cannot interfere with what happens in his spiritual life.

In these periods, when your spirits have fallen, you have to treat yourself as an ill man.

A wise man has doubts even in his best moments. Real truth is always accompanied by hesitations. If I could not hesitate, I could not believe.

—HENRY DAVID THOREAU

He who hesitates is not distanced from God; it is he who believes unhesitatingly in someone else's word that God exists or does not exist who is far from God.

September 17

The individual ownership of large areas of land is as unjust as the ownership of other people.

You cannot say that the existing laws regarding the possession of land are lawful. Violence, crime, and power have their source in these laws.

—HERBERT SPENCER

Private ownership of land came to be, not out of any natural relationships between people, but through robbery.

—HENRY GEORGE

The injustice of owning big pieces of land as private property, like any other injustice, is necessarily linked with many other injustices which are used to protect it.

September 18

Life's essence lies, not in your body, but in your conscience.

The divine spark lives in all of us, and perpetually strives toward its origin.

> —LUCIUS ANNAEUS SENECA

When you see that everything around you is impermanent, then you will perceive other, permanent and eternal things.

> —DHAMMAPADA, a book of BUDDHIST WISDOM

You cannot see the soul, but only the soul can truly see the essence of things.

> —The TALMUD

I call spirit that part of man which has independent existence and gives us the understanding of life.

> —MARCUS AURELIUS

Let your spiritual side guide your material side, and not the other way around. In order to improve his state, a person should strive for spiritual not physical perfection.

September 19

Nothing can enlighten people's lives and ease their burdens more than the understanding that they should serve God.

Religious disbelief and neglect is a great evil, but prejudice and lies are even worse.

—PLUTARCHUS

Life is short. Do not forget about the most important things in our life, living for other people and doing good for them.

—MARCUS AURELIUS

The Son of man came not to be ministered unto, but to minister, and to give his life as a ransom for many.

—MATTHEW 20:28

Pay goodness for evil. We should be like trees that give fruits to those who throw stones at them.

You should accept yourself, not as a master, but as a servant, and then all your bad feelings, your anxiety, alarm, uncertainty, and dissatisfaction will be changed into calmness and peace. You will be filled inside with a clear vision of your purpose, and with a great joy.

All good things can be achieved only with effort.

Bad things are easy to do, good things are done only with work and effort.
> —Dhammapada, a book of Buddhist wisdom

Enter by the narrow gate; for the gate is wide, and the way is broad that leads to destruction, and many are those who enter by it. For the gate is small, and the way is narrow that leads to life, and few are those who find it.
> —Matthew 7:13–14

The way to true knowledge does not go through soft grass covered with flowers. To find it, a person must climb steep mountains.

> —John Ruskin

Look for the truth; it wants to be found.

> —Blaise Pascal

A person cries out from pain when he takes up hard physical work after a period of idleness. Any rest from the struggle for spiritual improvement brings the same pain.

September 21

The most important and necessary expression of freedom is to give your thought a specific direction.

Work toward the purification of your thoughts. Without bad thoughts you will be incapable of bad deeds.
—CONFUCIUS

Everything is in heaven's power, except for our choice of whether to serve God or ourselves.

We cannot prevent birds from flying over our heads, but we can keep them from making nests on top of our heads. Similarly, bad thoughts sometimes appear in our mind, but we can choose whether we allow them to live there, to create a nest for themselves, and to breed evil deeds.
—MARTIN LUTHER

It is a sin, not only to do bad things, but even to think about bad things.
—ZOROASTER

September 22

Faith in the existence of eternity is our exclusively human quality.

The soul does not live in the body as in a house, but as in a tent, a place of temporary dwelling.

—INDIAN WISDOM

Who brought me into this world? According to whose command do I find myself at this exact place, during this particular time? Life is the remembrance of a very short day we spent visiting this world.

—BLAISE PASCAL

Mortal people cannot live long; we have only a few moments. But our soul does not age. It believes in eternal things, and it will live for all eternity.

—TORICLIDIS

Death is the destruction of the bodily organs with which I see my world during my life; the destruction of the glass through which I look at this world. The destruction of this glass does not mean the destruction of the eye itself.

Our understanding of eternity is the voice of God who lives within us.

No matter how big mankind's store of knowledge seems to me in comparison with our previous ignorance, it is only an infinitely small part of all possible knowledge.

Socrates did not have the weakness of many scholars, the desire to know about all possible things, to learn the origins and explanations of things—what the Sophists call "the nature of things"—and to uncover the origins of the celestial bodies. Socrates said, "Is it true that people are so concerned with these earthly things? People wrongly think that they should know everything. They think that they can despise the most necessary and important fields of knowledge, and penetrate the mysteries that do not belong to us."

—XENOPHON

Not only is real science not hostile to religion, in fact real science always supports it.

—JOHN RUSKIN

Knowledge is limitless, and the most scholarly and educated person is as far from true knowledge as an uneducated peasant.

—JOHN RUSKIN

We cannot imagine the scope of our ignorance, just as a blind man cannot imagine darkness until he can see.

—IMMANUEL KANT

It is better to know less than necessary than to know more than necessary. Do not fear the lack of knowledge, but truly fear unnecessary knowledge which is acquired only to please vanity.

It would be possible to eat meat if it were justified by any serious considerations. But it isn't; and meat eating is simply a bad thing that exists without any justification at all.

What nature of struggle for existence or kind of madness forces you to shed blood with your hands in order to eat animals? Why do this, if you have all the comforts of life?

—PLUTARCH

If it were not so blindly accepted as a part of our customs and traditions, how could any sensitive person accept the thought that in order to feed ourselves we should kill such a huge number of animals, in spite of the fact that our earth gives us so many different treasures from plants?

There is a big difference between, on the one hand, a person who does not have access to any food except meat, and on the other, an educated person of today who lives in a country which has vegetables and milk in abundance, and who is instructed against meat eating. The educated person sins greatly if he continues to behave in a way he knows is wrong.

September 25

Work is not a virtue, but it is the necessary condition of a virtuous life.

Hurried work done in irritation attracts the unfavorable attention of others. Real work is always quiet, constant, and inconspicuous.

It is not enough to be a hardworking person. Think: what do you work at?

—HENRY DAVID THOREAU

For every idle person, there is another person who works too much. For every person who eats to excess, there is another person somewhere who is hungry.

Much of the activity of idle people who pretend that they are busy with work is merely entertaining; it just adds a burden to other people. This can be said of all luxuriant entertainments.

September 26

All true wisdom and all true faith are clearly expressed in the same moral law.

All the world is subject to one law, and all thinking beings have the same basic intellect. Therefore, all wise men share the same idea of perfection.

—MARCUS AURELIUS

The more I dedicate my time to two things, the more they fill my life with ever-increasing pleasure. The first is the sky above me, and the second is the moral law within me.

—IMMANUEL KANT

Therefore all things whatsoever ye would that men should do to you, do ye even so to them: for this is the law and the prophets.

—MATTHEW 7:12

Moral law is so obvious and clear that even people who do not know the law have no excuse for violating it. They have only one recourse: to deny their intellect, which they do.

Blaming others is an entertainment which some people like and cannot restrain themselves from. When you see all the harm this blaming causes, you see that it is a sin not to stop people from practicing this entertainment.

If you want to blame me, you should not be with me. You should be inside me.

—ADAM MICKIEWICZ

Truth is achieved through discussion, but the wiser man stops the arguments.

Our greatest imperfections are in our inner vision. We are so shortsighted that we cannot see bad things in others, but we cannot find bad things in ourselves as well.

—EDWARD BROWN

As soon as you start blaming a person, stop yourself. Remember not to say something bad about someone, even if you know it to be true, and especially if you are not certain but are only repeating gossip.

Most people act, not according to their meditations, and not according to their feelings, but as if hypnotized, based on some senseless repetition of patterns.

You should be brave enough to use your own intellect, in life and in your education.

—IMMANUEL KANT

If, among the many voices which speak in my soul, I could only recognize my soul's true voice, then I would never make mistakes, and never do evil. This is why it is necessary to know yourself.

If you see that you are not behaving according to your inner desires, but because of some outer influence, stop and consider whether what drives you is good or bad.

Worse than all the troubles and horrors of war is the perversion of minds it causes. Armies exist and the cost of war exists, and people must wrestle to find explanations for what exists. War cannot be explained with the intellect, so to justify it, people create intellectual perversions.

Is there anything more absurd than a person having a right to kill me because we live on two opposite banks of the river, and our kings quarrel with each other?

—BLAISE PASCAL

The time will come when people will understand the stupidities of war.

—CHARLES RICHE

European countries have about four million people serving in the army. Two thirds of their budget are spent on military spending.

—GUSTAVE DE MOLINARI

Do not try to justify war or the existence of the military. If you try to apply logical thought to explain things that are evil, the effort will only prevent your intellect and poison your heart.

September 30

The more lonely a person is, the more clearly he can hear the voice of God.

The will to accomplish your good intentions depends on whether you voice them. You remember the things of which you spoke in your youth as if they were flowers that you tore out of a flower bed and threw away, and then saw lying on the earth, faded into the dirt.

In the important questions of life, we are always alone. Our deepest inner thoughts cannot be understood by others. The best part of the drama that goes on deep in our soul is a monologue, or, better to say, a very sincere conversation between God, our conscience, and ourself.

—HENRI AMIEL

Temporary solitude from all things in this life, the meditation within yourself about the divine, is food as necessary for your soul as material food is for your body.

October 1

A sage is not afraid of lack of knowledge: he is not afraid of hesitations, or hard work, but he is afraid of only one thing—to pretend to know the things which he does not know.

You should study more to understand that you know little.
— MICHEL DE MONTAIGNE

Never be ashamed to admit what you do not know.
— ARABIC PROVERB

Put everything to the test, hold fast to that which is good.
— I THESSALONIANS 5:21

Real wisdom comes, not from knowing what is good and what should be done, but from knowing which is the better thing and which is the worse, and therefore, what should be done and what should be done later.

To be wise one must study both good and bad thoughts and acts, but one should study the bad first. You should first know what is *not* clever, what is *not* just, and what is *not* necessary to do.

October 2

Religion is that which tells a person who he is and what the nature of the world in which he lives is.

We should teach our children those principles that are common to all religions—Buddhist, Muslim, Christian, Jewish, and so on, that is, for the moral science of love and the unification of all people.

Most people do not listen to God but adore him. It is better not to adore but to listen.

Moral teaching is not complete if it is not religious, but religious teaching is useless if it is not based on morality, that is, if it does not lead to a good life.

October 3

Big wealth will not give you satisfaction. The more your wealth grows, the more your requirements grow with it.

It is difficult if not impossible to find some reasonable limit for acquiring more and more property.
                                        —ARTHUR SCHOPENHAUER

You should acquire the kind of wealth which cannot be stolen from you by thieves, which people in power cannot take from you, which will stay with you even after your death, never diminishing and never disappearing. This wealth is your soul.

                                        —INDIAN PROVERB

There are two ways not to suffer from poverty. The first is to acquire more wealth. The second is to limit your requirements. The first is not always within our power, but the second is always in our power.

October 4

Real love refers not just to love for a particular person but to the spiritual state of loving everyone.

To love means to live within the lives of those whom you love.

Do not force others to love you; just love others, and you will be loved.

A holy person lives in the world, but he is concerned most of all about his attitude to people. He can feel all people, and he can sense all people, and all people turn their ears and eyes to him.

—LAO-TZU

Without love nothing can bring you goodness, and every action inspired with love, even if it seems small and unimportant, will bring you some fruits afterward.

—From the BOOK OF DIVINE THOUGHTS

Religion is the highest form of love.

—THEODORE PARKER

The more a person expresses his love, the more people love him; and the more people love him, the easier it is for him to love others. In this way, love is eternal.

October 5

Your spirit must constantly assert itself because your body is constantly exerting itself. As soon as you stop working at your spirit, then your body will have complete power over you.

What is not clear should be cleared up. What is not easy to do should be done with great persistence.

—CONFUCIUS

We suffer from our vices, and try to struggle with them, and the reason for this struggle is that we are not perfect. But our salvation is in this struggle with vices, and if God were to take away our ability to fight our vices, then we would be left with them forever.

—BLAISE PASCAL

A good thing is always done with an effort, and when the effort is repeated several times, then a good thing becomes a habit.

Do not detest any action which helps you to achieve good, or even more importantly—which can prevent you from doing evil.

October 6

Illness should be viewed as a natural condition of life.

Neglecting your health can prevent you from serving people, and too much attention to your body and its health can bring the same results. In order to find the middle way, you should take care of your body only to the extent that doing so helps you to serve others, and does not stop you from serving them.

No illness can prevent a person from what he has to do. If you cannot work, then give your love to people.

Illnesses of the mind are much more dangerous than illnesses of the body.

—MARCUS TULLIUS CICERO

Do not be afraid of illness, and do not think that being ill frees you from your moral requirements.

October 7

You can call God by various names, you can avoid his name altogether, but you cannot avoid accepting his existence. Nothing exists here if God does not exist.

All I know I know because there is God, and I know Him because He gives me the knowledge of everything.

Let us think about God, remember Him, and talk to Him as often as we can.

—EPICTETUS

God is not an idol; he is an ideal which we should strive for in our everyday life.

—LUCY MALLORY

It is very important to remember God, not necessarily with words, but in the sense of being aware of Him following your actions, supporting them or criticizing them. Russian peasants have a saying: "Do you remember God?"

October 8

Only people who have never thought about life's most important issues can believe that everything is possible for the human intellect .

There are three types of people. First, there are people who do not believe in anything; then, there are people who believe only in those teachings they were brought up to believe. Finally, there are people who believe in those things which they understand with their hearts, and this last group of people is the wisest and most resolute.

All beginnings are mysteries, the mystery of creation.

—HENRI AMIEL

Contemporary science cannot teach you about God and His virtues. The sciences cannot make you virtuous, but they help you on your way.

—LUCIUS ANNAEUS SENECA

Do not pretend to understand something that you do not. It is one of the worst possible things to do.

October 9

A person who comes into an understanding of the life of his spiritual self cannot fear evil, either in life or in death.

That which is born of the flesh is flesh; and that which is born of the Spirit is spirit. Marvel not that I said unto thee, Ye must be born again. The wind bloweth where it listeth, and thou hearest the sound thereof, but canst not tell whence it cometh, and whither it goeth: so is every one that is born of the Spirit.

—JOHN 3:6–8

The souls of wise people look to the future state of their existence; all of their thoughts are concentrated toward eternity.

—MARCUS TULLIUS CICERO

There is not a single soul that can be good without God.

—LUCIUS ANNAEUS SENECA

Salvation in all things lies in their spirituality. Evil cannot touch a person who knows his spirituality.

October 10

A man is both an animal and a spiritual being at the same time. As an animal, a man is afraid of death; as a spiritual being he does not experience death.

In the last moments before death, the soul leaves the body. It unites with the limitless, timeless, and eternal soul and transforms into another form, we know not which. After death, our body is left behind, and it becomes only an object for observation.

Death marks a change, it marks the disappearance of the dwelling place of your conscience. The conscience itself cannot be destroyed by death, in the same way as the change of a theater set cannot destroy a spectator.

Perhaps you fear the changes that death will bring?

But a similar great change already happened at the time of your birth, and nothing bad came out of it.

October 11

Most people are proud, not of those things which arouse respect, but of those which are unnecessary, or even harmful: fame, power, and wealth.

There is no worse scoundrel than he who, when he looks around himself at other people, can always find an even worse scoundrel than himself; and therefore, can be quite satisfied with himself.

A person who loves himself has the advantage of having very few competitors.

There is no wisdom in he who thinks that he is wise.

A selfish person is always limited. And one is connected with the other: he is selfish because he is limited; he is limited because he is selfish.

A proud person initially causes other people to think that he has more importance than he actually has, but when this influence disappears, as it always does, he becomes only the object of jokes.

October 12

Any departure from accepted traditions and customs requires a large and serious effort, but true understanding of new things always requires such an effort.

A society says to a man: "Think as we think, believe in what we believe, eat and drink what we eat and drink, and dress in the way we dress."

—LUCY MALORY

You should behave as you think is good, but not following the advice of the crowd.

—RALPH WALDO EMERSON

It is bad to irritate people by stepping back from their customs and traditions, but it is even worse to deny the requirements of your conscience and intellect by following the customs of the crowd.

October 13

A state system, no matter what kind of state system it is, functions at a far remove from the requirements of Christianity.

In those countries where wise people are in power, their subjects do not notice the existence of their rulers.

—Lao-Tzu

State violence cannot be destroyed by decree, only by truth and love. Maybe state violence was necessary for previous generations; maybe it is even necessary now, but people should conceive of a kind of future government in which violence will not be necessary.

You should live in such a way that violence is not necessary for you.

October 14

People are taught to speak, but their major concern should be how to keep silent.

If your tongue speaks good, there is nothing better in the world; if your tongue speaks evil, there is nothing worse.

—The TALMUD

I have spent all my life amongst wise people, and I found nothing better than silence in this world. If a word costs one coin, then silence costs two. Silence suits clever people, and it suits wise people even more.

—The TALMUD

Let your tongue become accustomed to the words "I do not know."

—EASTERN WISDOM

Keep silent. Give rest to your tongue more often than to your hands. You will never regret that you have kept silent, but you will often regret that you spoke too much.

Your chief task in life is the care of your soul. You should care for your soul and work to improve it, and you can improve it only with love.

The meaning of life lies in two major areas: your personal perfection and service to other people. You can serve while you are moving toward perfection, and you can move toward perfection by serving people.

When I talk of moving toward perfection, I mean moving from a material to a spiritual plane, a plane of goodness, without time or death.

Only one step lies between a five-year-old child and a man of my age. Between a newborn baby and a five-year-old child lies a huge distance. Between a fetus and a newborn baby lies an abyss; and between nonexistence and a fetus lies not only an abyss, but a gulf that surpasses comprehension.

From childhood to death, humans, no matter their lot in life, should strive to grow to get closer and closer to the spiritual life. Strive to learn what God wants, and your life will become filled with freedom and joy.

October 16

God is in all of us, and it is possible for all of us to find and understand him there.

To know yourself is to discover the good that lies within.

God is close to us, he is with us: the divine spirit is inside of us. If he were not, the power to be good would be beyond our reach. A person cannot be good without God.

—Lucius Annaeus Seneca

If you are going through a hard time, work harder to understand God; as soon as you understand Him, all difficult things will become easy, and you will feel love and joy.

If a person does not feel a divine force within himself, this does not mean that a divine force does not exist in him, but that he has not yet learned how to recognize it.

If there are people and there is God, then there are relationships between God and people. These relationships are changing with time, and mankind's religious conceptions are constantly evolving, constantly improving, becoming more clear and easily understood with the passage of time.

Religious conscience of mankind is not rigid, it is changing all the time, becoming purer and clearer.

God is spirit and part of this spirit lives inside me and gives sense to my life.

There is much good to be learned from the Koran, from the Buddhists, from Confucius, from the Old Testament, from the Indian Upanishads, and from the New Testament. But the closer a religious thinker or philosopher is to us in time, the more he can help us draw from these teachings in the light of our present-day lives.

October 18

The past no longer exists; the future has not yet come; there is only the present. And only in the present can the divine nature of the free human soul be manifested.

Then Jesus said unto them, Yet a little while is the light with you. Walk while ye have the light, lest darkness come upon you: for he that walketh in darkness knoweth not whither he goeth.

—JOHN 12:35

Everyone knows that our habits are improved and strengthened through their exercise. In order to be a good walker, you need to walk a lot; in order to be a strong runner, you need to run frequently; in order to be a perceptive reader, you ought to read as much as you can. The same is true of your soul: if you become angry, you must know that you not only perform evil, but you also create an evil habit, and you increase your potential for further evil.

—EPICTETUS

If you want to do a good deed, do it now. The time will pass, and you will not have the chance again.

October 19

The meaning of life is revealed to those who are ready to accept the things which will be revealed. And it is he who has already decided that he will accept the truth as it is, and not the truth itself, which will change the way of life he has been accustomed to.

Who am I? What should I do? What should I believe in and what should I hope for? All of philosophy is in these questions, said the philosopher Lichtenberg. But among all these questions, the most important one is that which is in the middle. If a person knows what he should do, he will understand everything which he should know.

Woe to the people who look without understanding, who do not know their foundations.
—After the Talmud

Every bird always knows where to make her nest. And if she knows how and where to make her nest, this means that she knows her purpose in life. And why does man, who is the wisest among all creatures, not know that which any bird knows, that is, his purpose in life?
—Chinese wisdom

The real meaning of life is not possible to embrace, if you are looking for the universal meaning of life. And at the same time it is so simple that it can be explained to fools and to infants when what to know is what you should do as an individual.

October 20

The life of man is filled with intellect only when the fulfillment of your duty is understood. We all know for sure that death waits for us. We do not know when, just as we do not know where we came from.

—HENRY GEORGE

Virtue is a service which a person should do for himself. If there were no heaven and no God who ruled this world, even then virtue would be the necessary law of life.

—INDIAN WISDOM

When you approach a man, you should think not about how he can help you, but how you might serve and help him.

We have the necessary law for all our actions, and this law cannot be restricted by any power. The fulfillment of this law is possible even in prison, and under the threat of tortures and death.

Look for a kind life which is in harmony with the will of God, and then you will fulfill the duty of your life.

October 21

In the same way as the storm troubles and muddies the waters, so too passions trouble our souls and interfere with our understanding of this life.

People with great and wonderful souls are always quiet and happy. Those people who do not have spirituality are always unhappy.

—CHINESE PROVERB

Do not be concerned too much with what will happen. Everything which happens will be good and useful for you.

—EPICTETUS

A person will understand his place in the world only when he understands his soul.

—CHINESE WISDOM

Real power is not in momentary desires, but in complete calmness.

Complete outer calmness is impossible. But when there are some calm periods, we should appreciate them and make them last longer. This is the time when useful thoughts appear; they become stronger and guide us in life.

Make sure that you do not gossip about your brother.

Time passes, but the words which you say will remain.

To stop your tongue from talking too much is a sign of great virtue.

The human soul, not by itself, but by some power, is pushed closer and closer to truth and goodness, and the better we understand this, the more humble we will be.

—MARCUS AURELIUS

If you think that it is necessary to judge your neighbor, then say this looking directly into his eyes, and say this in such a way that you do not create animosity.

October 23

Conscience is the understanding of the divine beginning which lives in us.

Conscience is the real judge between good and bad, conscience is what makes a person similar to God, and conscience is the greatest advantage of human nature. Without conscience there would be nothing that would raise us above the animals, and people would move from one lie to another.

—JEAN JACQUES ROUSSEAU

The purpose of your life is not to do as the majority does, but to live according to the inner law which you understand in yourself. Do not act against your conscience or against truth. Live like this, and you will fulfill the task of your life.

—MARCUS AURELIUS

You cannot fight with the requirements of conscience. These are the rules of God, and it is better to submit to them.

October 24

If the foundations of our life were not of the same nature in all of us, then we would not be able to explain to each other those feelings of compassion which we really experience.

Compassion expressed in response to rage is the same as water for fire. When you are in a rage, try to feel compassion for the other person, and then your rage will disappear.

—After ARTHUR SCHOPENHAUER

There are many people who are more unhappy than you. This message cannot be a roof under which you may live, but it will be enough of a roof under which you may hide from storms.

You hide from your misfortunes. But if you knew what other people suffered, then you would not complain about your own.

—SOLON

Real compassion begins only when you put yourself in the place of those who suffer, and you feel real suffering.

October 25

A person can understand his purpose in the same way as he understands his dignity. Only a religious person can understand his purpose in life.

A king asked a holy man, "Do you remember about me?" The holy man answered, "Yes, I think about you, when I forget about God."

—Muslih-ud-Din Saadi

We fulfill the law of God when we feel the lives of others as our own life.

—Giuseppe Mazzini

The freedom of a person is a great thing, and even the freedom of a whole nation begins from the freedom of a single individual.

You should respect freedom in yourself, and in your neighbor, and in all people.

Only he who understands himself as a spiritual being can understand the spiritual dignity of other people. Such a person will not lower himself with any act which is not worthy of a spiritual person.

October 26

For the moral, spiritual life, the importance of things is measured not by their material value, but by their level of goodness.

The majority of people want to do something unusual and difficult in order to improve their lives, but they would be better to purify their wishes, and improve their inner selves.

The second things are much more important than the first.

—After FRANÇOIS FÉNELON

A person understands himself not through thoughts, but with actions. It is only through making an effort that a person will understand his worth.

—JOHANN WOLFGANG VON GOETHE

To move yourself from the material to the spiritual means to do only spiritual things. My material body pulls my inner self to itself, but I try to separate my spiritual self from the material body. Though I use my body, I live within my spiritual life, which is my real life.

October 27

Real religion cannot be opposed to intellect.

Do not believe that in religion you cannot trust your intellect. The force of our intellect must support the foundations of every real faith.

—WILLIAM ELLERY CHANNING

If God, the object of our faith, is higher than our understanding, and if you do not understand Him, it does not mean that you should not use your intellect trying to understand Him.

—FYODOR STRAKHOV

While ye have light, believe in the light, that ye may be the children of light. These things spake Jesus, and departed, and did hide himself from them.

—JOHN 12:36

In order to understand the truth, you should not suppress your intellect. On the contrary, you should purify your intellect, exercise it, and intellectually try and test everything which we can possibly put to the test.

October 28

Pain is the necessary condition of our body, and suffering is the necessary condition of our spiritual life, from birth to death.

—MARCUS AURELIUS

You should welcome everything which happens to you from birth to death, because the existence and the purpose of the world is in these cases.

—MARCUS AURELIUS

Only in the storm can you see the art of the real sailor; only on the battlefield can you see the bravery of a soldier. The courage of a simple person can be seen in how he copes with the difficult and dangerous situations in life.

—DANIEL ACHINSKY

Those things which we call happiness and those which we call unhappiness are useful for us, especially when we see them as opportunities to try ourselves.

The legend about the wandering Jew who was suffering the punishment of eternal life is very true. In the same way, there is a legend about a man who was punished by being given a life without any suffering.

October 29

There is nothing more important than an example. It leads us to do good deeds which would be impossible without this example. Therefore, if we use dissipated or passionate or cruel people as examples, it destroys our soul. The contrary is also true.

Those who do not think independently are under the influence of somebody else who thinks for them. If you give your thoughts to somebody else, it is a more shameful slavery than if you give your body to someone to possess.

If you desire to follow someone as an example, as many other people do, first stop and think whether it is worthwhile to follow this general example.

Those who are not afraid of truly terrible things follow false examples and those people follow the path to destruction.

—DHAMMAPADA, a book of BUDDHIST WISDOM

Evil influence can be destroyed only by good influence. And the way to receive a good influence is to have a good life.

October 30

A sense of self-importance so high that it surpasses all limits is a mental illness called *mania grandiosa*.

People think that self-sacrifice violates your freedom. Those people do not know that sacrifice gives us complete freedom, and frees us from ourselves, from the slavery of our dissipation.

Our passions are the most terrible tyrants, and we can be the slave of them. Only self-sacrifice can free us from this slavery.

If you teach others how many insects exist in this world, or when you look at the spots on the sun, or when you write an opera or a novel—we do these things for different purposes. But to teach people goodness is done only for the purpose of self-sacrifice, service to others, and you cannot express this teaching without self-sacrifice. Christ gave his life on the cross for a great purpose, not in vain. And a sacrifice or suffering is never in vain, and it will triumph over everything.

October 31

Nothing can interfere with the growth of truth in the world: nothing except the wish to save old prejudices.

People say that God created mankind after his image. This means that man created God after his image.

—GEORGE LICHTENBERG

If we believe in the things we were taught, there is goodness and evil at the same time.

—HENRY GEORGE

Humanity slowly but ceaselessly moves forward to the better and better understanding of the meaning of this life.

Among the most terrible lies of all is to teach false faith to children.

Disrespect for traditions has not caused even one thousandth part of the great evil which was caused by the old prejudices, traditions, customs, and institutions which should not exist at present.

November 1

A man who considers himself the master of his own life can never be humble, because he thinks that he has no obligation to anyone. The man who considers service to God to be the purpose of his life is always humble, because he feels that he has never fulfilled his obligations.

And the apostles said unto the Lord, Increase our faith. And the Lord said, If ye had faith as a grain of mustard seed, ye might say unto this sycamine tree, Be thou plucked up by the root, and be thou planted in the sea; and it should obey you. But which of you, having a servant plowing or feeding cattle, will say unto him by and by, when he is come from the field, Go and sit down to meat? And will not rather say unto him, Make ready wherewith I may sup, and gird thyself, and serve me, till I have eaten and drunken; and afterward thou shalt eat and drink? Doth he thank that servant because he did the things that were commanded him? I trow not. So likewise ye, when ye shall have done all those things which are commanded you, say, We are unprofitable servants: we have done that which was our duty to do.

—Luke 17:5–10

Truly kind people forget the good things they have done in the past. They are so involved in the things they do now that they forget the things they have done before.

—Chinese wisdom

The better a person knows himself, the smaller and less significant he seems to himself, and the higher he elevates himself toward God.

—Thomas à Kempis

November 2

A deed done only to achieve glory is always bad, no matter what consequences it has. A deed motivated equally by the desire to achieve goodness and to achieve glory is indifferent. A deed is truly good only when its motivation is to fulfill the law of God.

If you care too much about being praised, in the end you will not accomplish anything serious. People have different values. You may say, "I want good people to value me," but you know you will respect only those who praise your actions.

We are not satisfied with our real life. We want to live an imaginary life, a life in which we seem different in the eyes of other people than we are in reality.

—BLAISE PASCAL

Let the judgments of others be the consequence of your deeds, not their purpose.

To live only for God, you should do good works which no one will ever discover. Do so, and you will experience a special joy.

November 3

There is only one real law, the law of God, which is the same for all of mankind. Human law can be valid only when it is in harmony with the law of God.

The first and most difficult obstruction to the fulfillment of the law of God is the fact that our society's existing laws are completely opposed to this law.

Those human laws are good which are based on the law of God. Those human laws are bad which contradict the laws of God; we should change these laws.

—GIUSEPPE MAZZINI

In order to study the most important questions of life, everyone should destroy the prejudices and lies which were created by previous centuries in relation to all serious questions in life.

The law of God contradicts human law. So what should we do? Should we hide the law of God and proclaim human law? People have done this for almost nineteen centuries, and the contradiction becomes stronger and stronger. There is only one solution: to replace the existing laws with the law of God.

Debates conceal the truth more often than they reveal it. Real truth should be revealed in solitude. When it is revealed, it becomes clear to you that you can accept it without any argument or discussions.

He has power who can keep silent in an argument, even though he is right.

You should abstain from arguments. They are very illogical ways to convince people. Opinions are like nails: the stronger you hit them, the deeper inside they go.

—DECIMUS JUNIUS JUVENALIS

If you live alone, think about your own sins; if you are in society, forget about the sins of others.

—CHINESE WISDOM

The more urgently you want to speak, the more likely it is that you will say something foolish.

November 5

Thought is the glorification of truth; therefore, bad thoughts are those which have not been thought through to the end.

In order that a lamp can give good light, you should put it in a place protected from the wind. If the light is in the wind, then it will leave long, trembling shadows. So too will bad thoughts drop shadows on the white surface of your soul.

—INDIAN WISDOM

Establish your purpose when you are alone and without temptations.

—JEREMY BENTHAM

Meditation is the way to eternity; lightheartedness is the way to death. Those who meditate never die; those who are lighthearted remind me of death.

—BUDDHIST WISDOM

You cannot send away a bad thought when it appears in your mind, but you can create other thoughts which will weaken or destroy this bad thought. For example, I may imagine that your friend or neighbor has some drawback, and I may not be able to banish this thought, but when I concentrate on the thought that criticizing another person is bad because I am not perfect, and he has the same God within him as I have within me, then I cannot stop loving this person.

November 6

Blaming your neighbor is harmful, both for you and for others.

Yesterday at a party, when a guest said good-bye and departed, everyone who was left started to slander him. The same thing happened to the second person when he left, and to all the guests, one after another, as they left. The last guest said, "Let me stay here and spend the night. I saw that all the people who left suffered and I am afraid for myself."

Be strict to yourself, and forgive others, and then you will have no enemies.

—CHINESE WISDOM

I once met an old man who spoke very slowly, pausing for several seconds between his words. He did this because he was afraid to sin with his words.

Let us forgive each other. If we can forgive each other, then we can live in peace.

A word is an expression of thoughts; thoughts are the expression of divine force. Therefore, words should correspond to our true meaning. Speech can be indifferent, but it should not be an expression of evil.

November 7

You can look at life as death, and death as an awakening.

I cannot stop thinking that I was dead before I was born, and at my death I will return to the same state.

—GEORGE LICHTENBERG

I do not regret that I was born here and that I lived part of my life here, because I lived in a way that I think was useful. When the end comes, I will leave my life in the same way, as if I leave an inn and not my home, because I think that my stay in this life is temporary and that death is only a transfer to another state.

—MARCUS TULLIUS CICERO

Even if I err in saying that the soul is eternal, nevertheless I am happy that I made this mistake. And while I am alive, not a single person can take away this assurance which gives me complete calmness and great satisfaction.

—MARCUS TULLIUS CICERO

We ask the wrong question when we say, "What will happen after death?" When we speak about the future, we speak of time, but when we die, we leave time behind.

November 8

We come to a right understanding of our life in relation to God in the same way we understand our relation to the world and to its things. Without conscience, we would never know anything about God.

The question is whether the intellectual one, without the heart, can understand God. The truth is that if our heart understands God our intellect will then start to seek Him.

—GEORGE LICHTENBERG

The basic foundation of the understanding of God is inside of us.

—WILLIAM ELLERY CHANNING

A good worker probably does not know the details of the life of his master. Only a lazy worker tries to do nothing except find out more about his master's way of life, tastes, and preferences in order to please him. The same is true of a person's attitude to God. It is important to accept Him as your master and to know what He wants you to do. I may never know the answers to the questions "What is He?" and "How does He live?" I will never find out because I am not equal to Him. I am His worker, not His master.

Every person understands God in different ways, but people fulfill His will in the same way.

November 9

Self-admiration is the beginning of pride. Pride is dissipated self-admiration.

Those who do not hate their own selfishness, their placing of themselves higher than the rest of the world, are blind, because this action contradicts the truth.

—BLAISE PASCAL

The lighter and less dense a substance is, the less space it occupies. The qualities which a proud person attributes to himself can be compared to this.

There are many people who claim to be teachers of others who should themselves be taught first of all.

—EASTERN WISDOM

The most important thing in life is the path to perfection, and what kind of perfection can exist if a person is proud and satisfied with himself?

November 10

From the first moment the members of a religious gathering said, "The Holy Spirit is among us," when they claimed theirs the highest authority above all other authorities, when they accepted the results of their own meditation as more worthy than the divine spark that exists in every person (that is, the intellect and the conscience), from this time, a great lie originated, a lie which deceives the bodies and souls of many people, which has destroyed millions of human beings, and which continues its terrible work.

In 1682, a Dr. Leyton, a respected citizen of England who wrote a book criticizing a bishop, was put on trial and severely punished. First he was harshly beaten, then one ear was cut away. After several days he was beaten again, though the injuries on his back had not healed; then they cut off his second ear, and tore off his nose. This was done in the name of Christianity.

—RANDALL THOMAS DAVIDSON

Christ never founded any church, never created any state, never passed any law, never established any government or other authority. He wanted to put the law of God into the hearts of people, to make them self-governed.

—HERBERT NEWTON

If there is a true church, the people who are inside it cannot see it from the outside.

November 11

Moral perfection is the impossible goal, but moving to it is the law of human life.

Some people say, "Man is selfish, greedy, and dissipated, and cannot be kind to other people." This is not true. We can be good. Feel in your heart the kind of person you should be; this feeling will give you power.

A woman accidentally dropped a precious pearl into the sea, and she started to scoop ocean water with a spade, one cup after another. A sea-sprite came to her and said, "When will you stop scooping up water?" The woman said, "When I have taken all the water from the sea, and retrieved my pearl from the bottom." Then the sea-sprite retrieved the pearl and returned it to her.

Outer consequences are not in our power to control; it is only possible to make an effort, and inner consequences always follow from our effort.

The land is the general and equal possession of all humanity, and therefore cannot be the property of individuals.

My intellect teaches me that land cannot be sold.

—BLACK HAWK

The land shall not be sold for ever: for the land is mine; for ye are strangers and sojourners with me.

—LEVITICUS 25:23

To be honest, the earth has two masters: the first is almighty God and the second are his sons; all the people who have worked and will work on it.

—THOMAS CARLYLE

All people, from the first, and without any judicial act, should possess the earth. They should be able to live where nature and chance have brought them.

—IMMANUEL KANT

The possession of land as property is one of the most unnatural crimes there is. We cannot see the horror of this crime because in our world it is accepted as law.

November 13

Self-perfection should be one's primary motivation. If you are truthful to yourself, you will never be satisfied with yourself.

A person should always develop his ability to do goodness. Make yourself better; this should be every person's goal.

—IMMANUEL KANT

The first rule of achieving goodness is this: think only about self-perfection, and do so without thought to being praised by others.

—CHINESE WISDOM

He who moves from doing bad deeds to doing good deeds enlightens this world like the moon coming out from behind the clouds. This is the best thing in the world; this is the first step toward divinity.

—DHAMMAPADA, a book of BUDDHIST WISDOM

Those who live life in perfection look only forward; those who have stopped moving forward look back on their achievements.

Dissatisfaction is a necessary condition of intellectual life. It is only this dissatisfaction that pushes you to work.

November 14

The most important knowledge is that which guides the way you lead your life.

It is harmful to eat if you are not hungry. It is even worse to have sex if you lack desire. But even more harmful is to try to think when you do not wish to, or to be engaged in meaningless intellectual activity. Many people do so when they want to improve their position.

Your will is not good until you have changed the habits of your intellect, and they will improve only when they follow the eternal laws of life.

—LUCIUS ANNAEUS SENECA

Only those who have real knowledge know what to do.
—INDIAN WISDOM

What is important in knowledge is not quantity, but quality. It is important to know what knowledge is significant, what is less so, and what is trivial.

The joy of wealth is inconstant.

Wherever your heart is, there will be your treasure. The heart of a person whose major treasure is wealth is buried in filth.

Is it true that people were created to collect more and more gold? No. God created people after His own image; He created you so that you could fulfill his will.

—SAINT JOHN CHRYSOSTOM

Why should a person be rich? Why should he have expensive horses, rich clothes, wonderful rooms, and the leisure to visit public places of entertainment? Because he does not have enough thoughts to accompany his intellect. Give this person the inner work of his intellect, and he will be happier than the richest man.

—RALPH WALDO EMERSON

For those who live a spiritual life, wealth is not only unnecessary but uncomfortable. It stops the development of one's real life.

November 16

Faith answers those questions to which the intellect cannot find answers, but which must be asked.

There is only one true religion, though there are many different faiths.

—IMMANUEL KANT

It is only faith which creates the powerful convictions, the energy, and the unity which can cure society.

—GIUSEPPE MAZZINI

We have only one sinless guide, a universal spirit which gets into all of us though we are all individuals, and which gives us the urge to do all that is necessary. The same spirit which exists in a tree and pushes it to grow straight and to produce seeds exists in us, urges us to be closer to God, and brings us closer to each other.

When a person is alive, he believes; the closer his faith is to the truth, the happier his life. The further from the truth his faith is, the more unhappy he is.

Without faith he does not live; he dies a premature death or else kills himself.

November 17

We suffer from the past, and we spoil our future because we neglect the present.

The best the future can offer is dreams. There is only one thing which really exists: the present.

Be attentive to the present. Only in the present time can we understand eternity.

—After JOHANN WOLFGANG VON GOETHE

Use your body, your vessel, today; tomorrow it can be broken.

—The TALMUD

There is no past and no future; no one has ever entered those two imaginary kingdoms. There is only the present. Do not worry about the future, because there is no future. Live in the present and for the present, and if your present is good, then it is good forever.

If you have difficult times, if you suffer from the loss of loved ones or from fears about the future, remember that life exists only in the present and direct all your thoughts and memories to this present. All your anguish about the past and your worries about the future will disappear, and you will feel freedom and happiness.

You cannot measure good by either the feeling of need or sacrifice, but only by the communication with God which is established between the giver and the receiver.

Life alone is not good. Goodness exists only in a proper, virtuous life.

—LUCIUS ANNAEUS SENECA

It is not a virtue, but a kind of deceitful similitude, to fulfill our duty for the purpose of its reward.

—MARCUS TULLIUS CICERO

All people become closer, more or less, to one of two opposite limits: one is life only for oneself, and the other is life only for God.

I call this life a happy one in which I do one good deed after another, with no intervals between them.

—MARCUS AURELIUS

We do good only when we do not notice what we do, when we forget ourselves and live only in others.

November 19

A material evil done by a person does not return to the evildoer, but the evil feeling which was created by the sinful deed will fester in his soul and sooner or later make him suffer.

If in the morning a person wants to do evil unto others, evil will return to him by nightfall.

—INDIAN WISDOM

The evildoer harms himself first, before he harms others.
—SAINT AUGUSTINE

Every man becomes what he teaches others to be. Those who gain victory over themselves will gain victory over others. It is most difficult to achieve victory over oneself. Every man has power only over himself.

—DHAMMAPADA, a book of BUDDHIST WISDOM

There is no material goodness which can restore the soul after the damage done by the evil which you create.

Remember: Those who suffer through to the end will be saved. Very often a person becomes desperate or even stops in his purpose when only a small effort is needed to achieve it.

But beware of men: for they will deliver you up to the councils, and they will scourge you in their synagogues; And ye shall be brought before governors and kings for my sake, for a testimony against them and the Gentiles. But when they deliver you up, take no thought how or what ye shall speak: for it shall be given you in that same hour what ye shall speak. For it is not ye that speak, but the Spirit of your Father which speaketh in you.

—MATTHEW 10:17–20

Right cannot be defeated, because it is done not by your will but according to the eternal laws of God.

—THOMAS CARLYLE

Persecution and suffering are the necessary conditions of the fulfillment of Christian law. Persecution is precious because it reveals whether a person lives with real faith.

Do not seek love in other people, and do not complain about the absence of their love for you. Some people love wrong, not right; therefore, try to please God, rather than people.

November 21

There is no deed in this life so impossible that you cannot do it. Your whole life should be lived as an heroic deed.

Every time you wake up and ask yourself, "What good things am I going to do today?" remember that, when the sun goes down at sunset, it will take a part of your life with it.

—INDIAN PROVERB

The virtue of a person is measured not by his outstanding efforts, but by his everyday behavior.

—BLAISE PASCAL

I am the tool with which God works. My virtue is to participate in this work, and I can do so if I keep the instrument which is given to me, namely my soul, in immaculate condition.

All things, even the most complicated things, become simple and clear if you separate them from other people and place them before God for judgment.

Other than our service to God, all our actions, whether we consider them important or not, are completely trivial. We may not know what the consequences of our actions will be, but we know what we should do.

November 22

The more busy you are with the improvement of your inner life, the more active you become in social life, helping other people.

It is as wrong for one person to rule many as it is for many to rule one.

—VLADIMIR CHERTKOV

What is truth? For the majority of people, truth is the majority of counted votes.

—THOMAS CARLYLE

When I sit on the seashore and listen to the waves beating on the sand, I feel free from any obligation, and I think that all the people of the world can change their constitutions without me.

—HENRY DAVID THOREAU

Never build, but always plant: in the case of the first, nature will interfere and destroy the creation of your work, but in the case of the second, nature will help you, causing growth in everything you planted. The same thing happens in your spiritual life: those things which are in harmony with the eternal laws of human nature will grow, but those things which correspond to the temporal wishes of people will not.

November 23

The question of life's meaning is a difficult problem which cannot be solved. So, too, is the question, "Why did God send us into this world?" But the meaning of life becomes very simple when a person asks himself, "What should *I* do?"

Your life may be cut short at any time; therefore, your life should have a deep purpose, a significance that will not depend on whether it is short or long.

There is only one way, if you want to live without understanding the meaning of your life: to become addicted to tobacco, alcohol, and drugs, and to live in the world of permanent entertainment.

This world is not a joke but rather a place for a trial, a way station to a better, eternal world. Our purpose is to make it a better and more joyous place to live, for those who live with us and those who come after us.

Our soul's perfection is our life's purpose; any other purpose, keeping death in mind, has no substance.

November 24

Helping others takes the form not only of physical aid, but of spiritual support for your neighbor. Stop blaming your neighbor and respect his human dignity.

Do not think that you are generous because you give your excess wealth to a poor person. Real generosity requires that you give this person a place in your heart.

—From the BOOK OF DIVINE THOUGHTS

He is virtuous who does not pay any attention to libel and evil speech.

You should be truthful; you should avoid wrath; you should give to those who ask, because they ask for small things. You will become holier by following these three paths.

—DHAMMAPADA, a book of BUDDHIST WISDOM

With humbleness, kindness, and self-sacrifice, you will take the weapon from any enemy. Any fire dies if there is insufficient wood.

—BUDDHIST WISDOM

Try not to hide the shameful memories of your sins in dark corners. On the contrary, keep them close to you and remember them, before you judge your neighbor.

War is murder. No matter how many people get together to commit murder or what they call themselves, murder is the worst sin in the world.

People of planet Earth are on a very low level of development. Every day in the newspapers you read the news about military treaties, about the preparations for war, for mass manslaughter. People do not understand that the life of each man is his own personal private property.

—CAMILLE FLAMMARION

The majority of people now understand not only the uselessness, but also the stupidity and cruelty of any war.

Until such time as people reject the power of government to govern, to tax, to legislate, and to punish, war will never stop. War is the consequence of the government's power.

November 26

Just as one candle lights another and can light thousands of other candles, so one heart illuminates another heart and can illuminate thousands of other hearts.

Beware of those who want to convince you that it is impossible to strive for good just because it is impossible to reach perfection.

—JOHN RUSKIN

Good books are a good influence. Good art is a good influence. Prayer is an influence as well. But the strongest influence is the example of a good life. A good life becomes a blessing for people, not only for those who live good lives but those who can see, know, and understand such lives.

It is difficult to bring people to goodness with lessons, but it is easy to do so by example.

—LUCIUS ANNAEUS SENECA

Beware of groups of people who are harmful for your soul. Try to avoid them. You should praise good company and seek it.

November 27

If a passion embraces you, you should remember that this passionate desire is not a part of your soul, but a dark covering which shuts out the true qualities of your soul.

You should be a lantern for yourself. Draw close to the light within you and seek no other shelter.

—BUDDHIST WISDOM

A person's soul may be compared to a transparent ball which is lit from the inside with its own light. This flame is not only the source of all light and truth, but it illuminates everything around you. In this state, the soul is free and happy. Only if it becomes addicted to anything outside you will it become troubled, darkened, and impenetrable. Distractions obstruct the light which shows you the way.

—MARCUS AURELIUS

The soul is a mirror in which you can see the reflection of divine intellect.

—JOHN RUSKIN

As soon as you feel passion, try to feel in yourself the understanding of your divine nature. As soon as you perceive that your divine nature is inactive and that you are possessed by passions, fight with these passions.

November 28

Life is not destroyed, only changed, by death.

The future is only an illusion inferred from our present state. What is important is not the length of life, but the depth of life. What is most important is not to make life longer, but to take your soul out of time, as every sublime act does. Only then does your life become fulfilled. And do not ask yourself questions about time. Jesus did not explain a thing about the eternity of life, but his influence brought people to the eternal.

—RALPH WALDO EMERSON

Faith in the eternity is given to us not in meditation, but in life.

It is not reasoning which will convince you of the necessity of life after death, but example: when you walk very close to a person, hand in hand, and this person disappears into an abyss, *over there,* stop in front of the abyss and try to look within it.

The level of fear you feel about death is the level of your understanding of life.

The less you fear death, the more you possess freedom, tranquillity, and an understanding of the greatness of your spirit and the joy of life.

The understanding of eternity is part of the nature of the human soul.

A word is an action.

Do not say words you do not feel, lest your soul be blackened with darkness.

> —From the BOOK OF DIVINE THOUGHTS

Your enemies can be more useful to you than your friends, because your friends can often pardon your weaknesses, but your enemies notice them and attract your attention to them.

Do not neglect the opinion of your enemies.

A wise man does not judge a person for his words, but at the same time does not neglect another person's words, even when these words are pronounced by an unworthy person.

> —CHINESE WISDOM

A person's tongue is a tool which is sufficient to transmit the ideas created by the human mind. But in the domain of true and deep feelings, our tongue is weak.

> —LAJOS KOSSUTH

Never is there a single instance when a lie can be justified.

When a humble person forgets himself, he is united with God.

People who try to force circumstances become their slaves. Those who use them become their masters.

—The TALMUD

There is nothing in this world more tender and more pliable than water, yet hard and rigid things cannot resist it.

Weakness defeats strength, tenderness defeats rigidity. Everyone knows this law, but no one acts upon it. The weakest in the world gain victory over the strongest; therefore, there is a great advantage in humility and silence. Only a few people in this world are truly humble.

—LAO-TZU

The more humble a person is, the freer and stronger he is.

December 1

A woman does not differ from a man in her chief mission. This mission is to serve God. The difference is in the method of this service. Though the mission of a woman's life is the same as that of a man's life and the service to God is fulfilled by the same means, namely love, for the majority of women the method of this service is more specific than for men. This is the birth and upbringing of new workers for the Lord throughout life.

If a woman's kindness is boundless, then her rage can also have no limits. A good wife is the best gift for a husband, and an evil wife is a terrible ulcer for a man.

—The TALMUD

The more beautiful a woman is, the more honest she should be because it is only through honesty that she can deal with all the evil and damage which her beauty can produce.

—GOTTHOLD EPHRAIM LESSING

It is not usually husbands who choose their wives, but wives who choose their husbands. In order to find a better father for her children, a woman must know good and evil. Therefore, women should have a good education first of all.

There is nothing more natural for a woman than self-sacrifice. Nothing can be more unpleasant in her than selfishness.

December 2

"Do not kill": these word refer not just to the killing of a person, but to the killing of anything which is alive. This commandment was written in the people's hearts even before it was heard on Mt. Sinai.

Whatever arguments they use against vegetarianism, men cannot prevent themselves from feeling compassion and disgust at killing sheep, cows, or chickens. Most people would rather stop eating meat than kill these animals themselves.

The more people become educated and the more our population grows, the more people will move from eating animals to eating plants.

Reading and writing do not educate if they do not help people to become kinder to all animals.

—JOHN RUSKIN

The stupidity, lawlessness, and harm, both physical and moral, of meat eating is so clear that meat eating is not supported by reasoning but by old traditions and prejudices. We should not even argue about the absence of logic in eating meat; it is self-evident.

December 3

Art is the activity whereby a person makes a conscious attempt to use the particular means at his disposal to transmit his feelings to others so that they feel them as intensely as he does.

In a true creation of art, there is not only no border between the work of art and the artist, but also between the work and the other people who experience it. The major attraction of real art lies in this unification.

A new work of art should bring a new emotion in our life.

Emerson said that music helps people to find the greatness in their souls. The same can be said about any form of art.

Contemporary artists and scholars do not fulfill and cannot fulfill their destinies, because they have transformed their duties into their rights.

December 4

It is not said by chance that the essence of divine law is to love God and your neighbor. Neighbors come and go, but God exists always. Therefore, a man can fulfill this law when he is alone in a desert, or when he is in prison. He can love God and God's manifestations even in his thoughts, memories, and imagination.

Remember that the spirit of God exists in every person, the same spirit that gives you life. Therefore you should not only love but respect the soul of every person as a holy place.

I do not grieve that a person dies, that he loses his money, his estate, or all his property, all that can belong to a man. But it is a great pity when a person loses his greatest possession, his human dignity.

—Epictetus

Do not do anything, either among others or alone, which is opposed by your conscience.

In our time, people forget that first of all they should respect the human being in themselves.

—Ralph Waldo Emerson

Beyond his duty to his neighbor, every person has an obligation to himself, as to the Son of God.

December 5

The longer mankind exists, the more liberated it becomes from prejudice and the more clearly it perceives the law of life.

Ours is the age of criticism.

Religion and law try to escape from criticism, religion by saying that it is divine and law by showing that it is powerful. But some suspicions arise from this escape, because we can respect only those things which stand up in free and public trial.

—IMMANUEL KANT

Study everything, and put intellect first.

—PYTHAGORAS

Do not be afraid of the way your intellect calls into question old stories and legends. The pure intellect cannot destroy anything without replacing it with the truth: this is one of its essential qualities.

December 6

We have misconceptions not because we think illogically but because we live our lives badly.

Ignorance cannot lead to evil, misconceptions lead to evil. It's not what people do know, it's what they pretend that they do.

—JEAN JACQUES ROUSSEAU

Every misconception is a poison: there are no harmless misconceptions.

—ARTHUR SCHOPENHAUER

One of the evil properties of man is that he loves only himself and wants goodness only for himself. But woe to him who loves only himself!

—BLAISE PASCAL

The fight between the spiritual and material inner nature goes on in everyone. Thus, all people have misconceptions, and many will always mistake them for the truth.

To feed the hungry, to clothe the naked, to visit the ill in the hospital—these are acts of mercy, but there is one charitable deed which cannot be compared to them: to free your brother from misconception.

December 7

Life consists of numerous invisible, imperceptible changes, changes that began at birth and end with death. It is not possible for us humans to observe them all.

Truly, truly, I say to you, unless a grain of wheat falls into the earth and dies, it remains by itself alone; but if it dies, it bears much fruit. He who loves his life loses it, and he who hates his life in this world shall keep it to life eternal.

—John 12:24–25

Life is changing all the time, and only the ignorant do not look into the depth of things.

—Lucy Malory

Why are you so afraid of change? Nothing in this world can be done without change. Only one rule should remain constant: do not do anything inhumane to others.

—Marcus Aurelius

Everything in this world blooms, grows, and returns to its roots. Returning to one's roots means becoming united with nature; becoming united with nature involves eternity. The destruction of your body holds no danger in itself.

—Lao-Tzu

Death is a change to a form with which our spirit is united. You should not confuse the form with those things with which it is united.

December 8

It seems so easy to fulfill the law of God that is expressed in the Christian teaching, but we are still so far from this fulfillment!

The law of right living is not immediately clear to the wise man, but it becomes much clearer when he follows it. The law of right living is immediately clear to the ordinary person, but it becomes less obvious when he tries to follow it.
—CONFUCIUS

There is only one eternal law. It does not change and it governs all people at all times.
—MARCUS TULLIUS CICERO

December 9

Man's purpose is to serve all mankind, not to serve only one man while doing harm to others.

For a Christian, the love of one's motherland can be an obstacle to the love of one's neighbor.

Lost souls escape their loss of control in patriotism.
—Dr. Samuel Johnson

Patriotism is not a virtue. Sacrificing your life for an institution which embodies prejudice cannot be your duty.

People do many bad things for selfish reasons; they do worse things for their families. But they do the worst in the name of patriotism, and they are made proud by these crimes: spying, unduly heavy tax collecting, sacrificing lives, and waging wars.

Loving your country and loving your family are both virtues that can become vices when they become overwhelming and damage your love for your neighbor.

December 10

One of the worst things possible is to follow the rule: "Be like everyone, follow the crowd."

Woe to the world because of its stumbling block! For it is inevitable that stumbling blocks come; but woe to that man through whom the stumbling block comes! And if your hand or your foot cause you to stumble, cut it off and throw it from you; it is better for you to enter life crippled or lame than having two hands and two feet, to be cast into the eternal fire.

—MATTHEW 18:7–9

One of the major obstacles impeding any positive future change in our lives is that we are too busy with our current work or activity. Levi quit his tax-work, Peter stopped fishing at a lake, Paul ceased being a priest. They all left their jobs because they thought it was necessary.

—JOHN RUSKIN

If a person's hand is not damaged, then it can withstand the bite of a poisonous snake. Its poison poses no danger to a healthy hand. Evil is harmless for him who is not an evildoer.

—BUDDHIST WISDOM

False shame is the devil's favorite emotion; it is even worse than false pride. Pride can support evil, but false shame stops goodness.

—JOHN RUSKIN

There is no evil in the world itself. All evil exists in our souls, and can be destroyed.

December 11

Nothing is more joyful than the labor of a farmer tilling the soil.

The best food is the food you or your children make by yourself.

—Mohammed

Those who provide for their own food by themselves deserve more respect than those who claim to be religious.

—The Talmud

Working on the land and making your own bread isn't necessary for all people, but no type of work is more important for humanity, and no type of work offers a greater degree of independence and good.

December 12

Kindness defeats everything and can never be defeated.

You can stand firm in a fight against everything except kindness.

—JEAN JACQUES ROUSSEAU

It is not the blaming of evil but the glorifying of goodness that creates harmony in our life.

—LUCY MALORY

If a good action has an ulterior cause, then it is not truly good. If it expects reward, it is not truly good. Good things are beyond reason and consequence.

In the same way that fireworks and torches cannot be seen in the light of the sun, the best intellect and the greatest beauty cannot be seen in the light of the kindness of a single heart.

—ARTHUR SCHOPENHAUER

The most tender plants can push their way through the hardest rocks, and it is the same with kindness. Nothing can stop a truly kind and sincere person.

—HENRY DAVID THOREAU

The person does not exist to whom you cannot do good.

—LUCIUS ANNAEUS SENECA

We do good to people not in hope of reward, but because we see the divine spirit within everyone.

The best and easiest way to thwart evil in this world is to respond to it with kind words, return an evil action with good.

December 13

True faith is faith only if the actions of your life are in harmony with it and never contradict it.

During the day you should behave in such a way that you can sleep at night in peace; and in your youth you should behave in such a way that you can live in your old age in peace.

—INDIAN PROVERB

Those who have weak faith themselves cannot arouse faith in others.

—LAO-TZU

Those who give second place to God in their hearts do not give Him a place at all.

—JOHN RUSKIN

We can never fully understand the final purpose of human life. A construction worker who works at a construction site can have no idea of the final form or general design of the large structure he builds, but he can know that he is working on something good, something beautiful, clever, and necessary, both for him and for the world. This is faith.

Do not believe in words, yours or others'; believe in the deeds.

December 14

A person who becomes close to God understands that God lives within him. Angelus, a mystical poet of the seventeenth century, said, "I see God with the same eye with which He sees me."

—HENRI AMIEL

The soul of a person is the lamp of God.

—The TALMUD

People do not know what God looks like but they live in Him and He in them.

—SUFI WISDOM, a mystical sect in ISLAM

Those who can raise their thoughts to heaven will always have clear days, because the sun always shines above the clouds.

If you are gnawed by desire or fear you must not believe in God, who is filled with love, and who exists in you. If you believe in Him, you know that you need not wish for anything because the wishes of God always come true; and you need never be afraid of anything, because God fears nothing.

The nature of a soul is so mysterious that no matter how hard we try to understand it, we will never be able to define it.

—HERACLITUS

Whatever may happen to you, you will never be unhappy if you understand your unification with God.

December 15

Only misconceptions need to be supported by elaborate arguments. Truth can always stand alone.

All goodness is as nothing compared to the goodness of truth; all sweets are as nothing compared to the sweetness of truth. The bliss of truth surpasses all other joys in the world.

—BUDDHIST WISDOM

A person cannot be completely truthful all the time, because different forces and aspirations fight within him, and sometimes he cannot express them, even to himself.

Misconceptions exist only for a finite period of time, but real truth remains as it always was, after all tricks, sophisms, and lies have withered away.

Learn what to do, think, and say the truth at all times. Only when you start to learn this can you understand how far we are from real truth.

Lies are always harmful to all living things.

No person is without sin; no person is completely truthful. It is not that one person is virtuous and truthful and another is sinful and deceitful; rather it's that one person strives to move toward truth and virtue and the other does not.

December 16

Only the spread of love between people can improve the existing social structure.

Love gives meaning to human life. This we have known since antiquity. But what is love? Many wise people throughout the ages have tried to solve this question.

If you raise people to praise only wealth, power, and glory, then naturally they will praise only these things. If you raise people to love the feeling of love, they will start to live in love.

—MEE-TEE, a student of CONFUCIUS

Only one clear quality marks an action as either good or evil: If it increases the amount of love in the world, it is good. If it separates people and creates animosity among them, it is bad.

The time is coming, a time of concord, harmony, forgiveness, and love. Depend on it. We must do everything in our power to bring this time closer, and to stop those things which delay its arrival.

December 17

Our understanding of ourselves as discrete beings separate from each other grows out of conditions of our life in time and space. The less we feel this separation, the more we feel our unification with all other living creatures, the lighter our load, and the more joyful our life will be.

For the body is not one member, but many. . . . And if one member suffers, all the members suffer with it; if one member is honored, all the members rejoice with it.
> —I CORINTHIANS 12:14, 26

A small branch cut off from a big limb is separated from the whole tree. In the same way when a person is in an argument with another person, he is separated from all humanity.

> —MARCUS AURELIUS

God created heaven and earth, but they lacked the ability to understand the happiness of their existence. Then God made creatures who could understand the happiness of their existence, and who could create a single body from all of its thinking parts. All people are members of this one body; in order to be happy, they should live in harmony with the will that governs its life. We should live in harmony with this great soul and love it more than we love ourselves.

> —BLAISE PASCAL

We manifest in love our understanding of the unity of our being with others, and in so doing we make our life greater. The more we love, the wider, larger, and more joyful our life becomes.

December 18

Mankind moves ceaselessly toward perfection, not of every person's accord, but through the efforts that some particular individuals make toward their personal perfection. The kingdom of God will be created by these individual efforts.

Do not be embarrassed by all your bad deeds, by all your misfortunes. Do not be embarrassed, but fight ceaselessly, bravely, and without hesitation, because the kingdom of God will come.

—F. ROBERT DE LAMENNAIS

We hear often that there is no use in working to improve our life, to fight evil, or to establish justice, because progress will occur by itself. Imagine that a boat floats along a river. Imagine that those who have sat by the oars and rowed tirelessly have stopped and gone ashore; and that the travelers who remain in the boat do not bother to take up the oars and push the boat further, but think that it will travel by itself, as before, into the future.

Life has no meaning without purpose. To lack purpose is to deny the existence of God and to admit that our life is an evil, stupid joke.

—GIUSEPPE MAZZINI

All our history proves that God may be understood, not by reasoning, but by submission to Him and obeyance to His laws. Only by doing this can we understand His will on earth.

—JOHN RUSKIN

Every person should make a small effort, even the smallest effort, to improve the general well-being of humanity.

December 19

Real goodness is in your hands. It follows a good person as a shadow follows its object.

Everything which can make us better and happier was given to us by God. If our conscience is clear, then nothing can harm us.

—Epictetus

They who have decided to dedicate their lives to spiritual perfection will never be dissatisfied or unhappy, because all that they want is in their power.

—Blaise Pascal

Happiness, pure happiness, is a virtue in itself.

—Benedictus Spinoza

The greater the effort a person makes to achieve pleasure, the less possible it is for him to possess real goodness, or love.

They who say that doing good causes them unhappiness either don't believe in God or aren't doing something that is truly good.

December 20

The real purpose of Christianity is obvious to all, and it is stronger than the lies which try to pervert it.

We should separate the religion that was taught by Jesus from the religion whose subject is Jesus. Then we will understand the real meaning of the New Testament and follow it.

—HENRI AMIEL

I see a new religion based on mutual trust, which appeals to our deepest selves, and which teaches that a person should love goodness without reward, and that the divine exists in everyone.

In different ways and in different tongues, all humanity repeats the words of the Lord's prayer, "Let thy kingdom come on earth as it is in heaven."

—GIUSEPPE MAZZINI

Do not think that you will personally see the coming of the kingdom of God. But have no doubt that it will come soon: it is coming closer and closer, without hesitation.

December 21

At the highest level of consciousness, an individual is alone. Such solitude can seem strange, unusual, even difficult. Foolish people try to escape it by means of various dissipations in order to get away from this high point, to some point lower, but wise people remain at this high point, with the help of prayer.

God wants us to fulfill his will here on earth, in our lives. But life's interests and passions distract us from this every minute. When we understand this, we can gird ourselves with the physical expression of our attitude to God, prayer.

A personality is a limitation and, therefore, God, as we understand Him, is not a personality. Prayer is our address to God and yet how can we address one who has no personality? I address God as if He were a person, though I know it is not so.

A person buried in a deep mine, freezing from the cold in deep ice, dying from hunger alone on the open sea, wasting away in solitude in a prison cell, or simply dying at home, deaf and blind—how could this person live out the remainder of his life if prayer did not exist?

How good a person feels when, exhausted from striving for goodness in his everyday life, he stretches out his hands to God.

—BLAISE PASCAL

One can live without prayer either when he is possessed by his passions or when his life is completely dedicated to God. But for a person who is fighting his passion and yet far from fulfilling his duty, prayer is a necessary condition of life.

December 22

Nothing seems to check the notion that the way to improve civilization is affected by changing its outer forms. This notion is false, and draws the activity of too many people away from effort that truly can improve our lives.

Civilization is first of all a moral thing. Without truth, respect for duty, love of neighbor, virtue, everything is destroyed. The morality of a society is alone the basis of civilization.

—HENRI AMIEL

The proper direction of man's thought is not toward the creation of new laws for government, but toward the acceptance of every person's moral dignity.

—EDMUND YATES

Socialism, when compared with Christianity, is a rather minor, secondary question about the material needs of the working class. It stands outside the basic questions of human life.

—FYODOR STRAKHOV

We should, first of all, understand that we are all children of the same father, and we should fulfill the same general law: live not for ourselves, but to help others be happy.

—GIUSEPPE MAZZINI

When we accept false and violent laws and submit to them, we can neither establish truth nor combat lies in this world.

December 23

Wisdom is understanding how eternal truth can be applied to life.

Socrates was the first who brought philosophy from heaven, distributed it among the people, and enticed them to study the science of life, human morals, and the consequences of good and evil.

Science is seldom connected with wisdom. A scholarly person knows many unnecessary things. A wise person knows few things, but all that he knows is necessary both for humanity and for himself.

He who understands his soul will understand the divine spark within himself.

—Marcus Tullius Cicero

Wise people cannot be sufficiently educated, and educated people cannot be sufficiently wise.

—Lao-Tzu

The goodness given to us by wisdom compares to all other knowledge in the same way that in a desert, a vessel filled with water compares to mountains of gold.

December 24

Starting from early childhood, as we age we feel the growth of our spiritual power and the diminution of our physical power.

Older people who live spiritual lives ever widen their spiritual horizons, and ever expand their consciences. Older people who live only a daily routine become more and more stupid over the years.

—The TALMUD

One becomes older in order to become kinder; there is no mistake which I have not already made.

—JOHANN WOLFGANG VON GOETHE

The growth and development of the soul is more important than power and glory.

—HENRI AMIEL

The growth of our physical energy prepares us for spiritual work, for serving God and mankind; this work starts when our body begins to fade away.

Grow spiritually and help others to do so; it is the meaning of life.

Terrible is the situation of those who cannot perceive spiritual growth in themselves. They can see only physical life, which will disappear in time.

When you understand your spiritual being and live with it, then instead of despairing you understand the joy that can never be destroyed, which always grows.

December 25

Kindness and virtue come from the heart, and should be performed without thought for the opinion of others, or of future rewards.

Virtue and charity start at home. If you have to go somewhere to display it, then it is not virtue.

Assistance given to the poor by the rich is too often just a gesture of politeness, not real charity.

Charity is good only when it comes as a sacrifice; only then do those who receive the material gift receive the spiritual gift too. If it is not a sacrifice but a discharge of excess, it can only irritate those who receive it.

December 26

Childhood is the period in which underlying convictions are formed. Therefore, the most important part of education is the selection of the things of which a child should be convinced.

Talking and reasoning does not even have one thousandth the influence a true example has. All lessons about how to behave are worthless when children see the opposite in real life.

What use is it for children when people only speak about goodness, but perform bad deeds in reality?

—GUSTAV STRUVE

The strong desire for a pleasant and ideal life is a child's worst misfortune. It is crucial that children should know how to work from an early age.

—IMMANUEL KANT

It is important to teach children kindness and simplicity in life and work. All of children's moral and spiritual education should be supported by your own good example. You should live virtuously, or at least try to do so; the success of your good life will educate your children.

December 27

All that we see and know does not exist in reality, because it is the product of our limited ability to understand reality.

Instead of saying that the world is reflected in our intellect, better to say that our intellect is reflected in the world.

—GEORGE LICHTENBERG

Old fortresses are destroyed, monuments to kings are demolished, old age ravages our bodies. Only the teachings of kindness are never ruined or affected by age.

As soon as a person truly looks at himself as only a physical body, then he sees an unsolved puzzle, a contradiction that cannot be unraveled.

In order to understand the true essence of a thing we must transform the physical into the spiritual.

December 28

Science is vitally important when it is harnessed to reveal the law of human life.

In order to accept the importance of science, we must prove that this activity is useful. Scientists usually demonstrate that they are doing something and that maybe sometime, someday, this could be useful for people in the future.

The universe is limitless, and impossible for anyone to understand. Therefore, we cannot completely understand the life of our own body.

—BLAISE PASCAL

"Science" is not quite the concept which people use this word to identify; it is the highest, most important, most necessary object of our understanding.

As long as there is violence, there will be war. One cannot defeat violence with more violence, only with nonresistance to and nonparticipation in it.

—LETURNO

If my soldiers started thinking, not a single soldier would remain in my army.

—FREDERICK II

The wild instinct of military murder has developed in humanity over the course of thousands of years, and has become rooted in our brains. We must hope that our society will be able to rid itself of this terrible crime.

With time I understand the army code that dictates that a sergeant is always right when he addresses a soldier, that a lieutenant is always right when he addresses a sergeant, and so on up to generals and marshals, even when a person says that two times two equals five. If you do not obey your superior, you are punished by death, or years in prison.

—EDWARD EKMAN

Wars can be stopped only if people are ready to be persecuted for not participating in them. This is the only way.

December 30

The understanding of the fraternity and equality of all people becomes more and more popular among mankind.

Do we understand our spiritual fraternity? Do we understand that we originated from one divine Father whose image we carry in ourselves and for whose perfection we strive? Have we accepted that there is the same divine life in all people, as well as in ourselves? And that this makes a natural and free bond among people?

—WILLIAM ELLERY CHANNING

We can love neither those whom we fear nor those who fear us.
—MARCUS TULLIUS CICERO

Family and motherland are but two circles that are part of the wider circle that is humanity. Those who teach morality and who limit one's duties only to family and country teach a selfishness which is dangerous for all of us.

The understanding of one's unity with all of humanity comes from the understanding of the divine beginning in us all, and gives all our greatest good. True religion creates this understanding, and different prejudices interfere with it—prejudice of state, nation, and class.

December 31

The past does not exist. The future has not begun. The present is an infinitely small point in time in which the already nonexistent past meets the imminent future. At this point, which is timeless, a person's real life exists.

"Time passes by!" we say. Time does not exist; only we move.

—After the TALMUD

Time is behind us, time is before us, but in the present there is no time.

I consist of spirit and body. Time affects the body, but the life of the spirit has no meaning either in the past or in the future. All its life is concentrated in the present.

—MARCUS AURELIUS

Divine spirit is eternal, it exists out of time. Limitless time and space are divided into small, limited parts to be used by limited beings.

—HENRI AMIEL

The soul is put into our body, so that it can understand the notion of date and time. It contemplates this fact and calls it "nature."

—BLAISE PASCAL

Time does not exist. There is only a small and infinite present, and it is only in this present that our life occurs. Therefore, a person should concentrate all his spiritual force only on this present.

THE NAME INDEX

WITH BRIEF BIOGRAPHIES
OF MAJOR PERSONALITIES

BROWN, EDWARD (1811–1891), British religious writer, bishop, August 30, September 27.

BUDDHA (563[?]–[?]483 B.C.), originally Siddharta Gautama, Indian mystic and founder of Buddhism, June 11.

BUDDHIST WISDOM, February 16; May 6, 12, 23; June 6; September 14; November 5, 24, 27; December 10, 15.

CARLYLE, THOMAS (1795–1881), British historian and journalist, January 21; February 29; April 14, 28; July 16; August 4; November 12, 20, 22.

CARPENTER, EDWARD (1844–1929), British writer, August 4.

CHANNING, WILLIAM ELLERY (1780–1842), American clergyman and writer, January 10, 15; February 10; April 10; June 15, 26; July 18, 29; August 23, 30; October 27; November 8, December 30.

CHERTKOV, VLADIMIR (1854–1936), Tolstoy's friend and publisher, November 22.

CHINESE PROVERB (WISDOM), January 3, 4, 13, 17; February 14, 27; March 13, 14, 28; April 25; May 13, 15, 17, 19; June 3, 7; July 5, 16, 20; August 1, 27; September 4, 13; October 19, 21; November 1, 4, 6, 13, 29.

CHRYSOSTOM, SAINT JOHN (347–407), Christian scholar, patriarch of Constantinople, January 26; March 17; June 9; September 12; November 15.

CICERO, MARCUS TULLIUS (106–48 B.C.), Roman philosopher and orator, January 30; February 12, 16; April 3, 24; May 4, 19; June 23; July 3, 19, 25; August 2; September 12; October 6, 9; November 7, 18; December 8, 23, 30.

COMB, ABRAHAM (1785–1834), British philosopher, August 14.

COMTE, AUGUSTE (1798–1857), French philosopher, March 20.

CONFUCIUS (551–479 B.C.), Chinese philosopher, January 11, 29; February 7, 14; April 2; May 3, 15, 20; June 14, 21; July 24; August 17; September 4, 13, 21; October 5; December 8.

CONSIDÉRANT, VICTOR (1809–1894), French socialist and philosopher, lived in America, September 14.

DANIEL, SAMUEL (1562–1619), British poet, October 28.

DAVIDSON, RANDELL THOMAS (1848–1930), British clergyman, November 10.

DEMOCRITUS (460–370 B.C.), Greek philosopher, May 7.

DEMOSTHENES (385–322 B.C.), Greek author and philosopher, June 25; September 12.

DESCARTES, RENÉ (1596–1650), French philosopher, May 29.

DHAMMAPADA, a book of BUDDHIST WISDOM, January 6, 23, 25; February 18; March 10, 29, 31; April 7, 11; May 7; June 6, 25; August 11; September 18, 20; October 29; November 13, 19, 24.

DUCLOS, JEAN FRANCE, September 2.

EASTERN WISDOM, January 5; March 29; April 18; May 3, 7; June 2, 13, 26; July 22; August 13; October 14; November 9.

ECKMAN, EDWARD (1638–?), Belgian writer, December 29.

EGYPTIAN WISDOM, May 8.

EL GAFFER, DAUD, May 13.

ELIOT, GEORGE (1819–1880), English novelist, March 11.

EMERSON, RALPH WALDO (1803–1882), American poet and essayist, January 1, 12, 15; March 21; April 3, 16, 23; May 13, 14, 28, 31; June 4, 12, 18, 27; July 10; August 11; October 12; November 15, 28; December 4.

EPICTETUS (c. 50–130), Greek philosopher, January 6; February 4; March 2, 30; April 27; May 1, 14; June 23; July 3; August 1; October 7, 18, 21; December 4, 19.

ERASMUS, DESIDERIUS (1466[?]–1536), February 12.

FÉNELON, FRANÇOIS (1651–1715), Roman Catholic theologian, October 26.

FLAMMARION, CAMILLE (1842–1925), French astronomer and writer, November 25.

FLÜGEL, EWALD (1863–1914), German American philosopher, January 2.

FRANCE, ANATOLE (JACQUES ANATOLE FRANÇOIS THIBAULT) (1844–1924), April 19; June 17.

FREDERICK II, December 29.

GARDUEN, HENRI HARDUIN, July 6.

GEORGE, HENRY (1839–1897), American scholar, reformer, and economist, January 16; March 23; April 14; September 17; October 20, 31.

GOETHE, JOHANN WOLFGANG VON (1749–1832), German poet, February 29; April 7; August 7, 25; October 26; November 17; December 24.

GOGOL, NIKOLAI (1809–1852), Russian novelist, January 5; March 10; May 10.

GOLDSTEIN, MIKHAIL (1853–1905), professor of St. Petersburg University in Russia, July 20.

GOSPEL OF SRI RAMAKRISHNA, THE, a book of HINDUISM, May 14; July 1.

HEINE, HEINRICH (1797–1856), German poet, January 31.

HERACLITUS (540–475 B.C.), Greek philosopher, January 20; December 14.

HERBERT, EDWARD (1582–1648), English philosopher, July 30.

HERZEN, ALEXANDER (1812–1870), Russian poet and writer, June 30.

HOLMES, OLIVER WENDELL (1809–1894), American journalist and poet, January 24.

INDIAN PROVERB (WISDOM), February 22; March 12; April 5, 22; May 18; June 6, 18, 23; July 15, 22; August 29; September 22; October 3, 20; November 5, 14, 19, 21; December 13.

ISLAMIC WISDOM, June 22.

JOHNSON, SAMUEL (1709–1784), British writer and lexicographer, December 9.

JEFFERSON, THOMAS (1743–1826), third president of the United States, January 7; September 5.

JUVENALIS, DECIMUS JUNIUS (c. 60–c. 140), Roman lawyer, November 4.

KANT, IMMANUEL (1724–1804), German philosopher, January 10, 15; February 11, 13, 19, 28; April 1, 2, 9; May 9, 19; June 13, 16, 18, 22; July 14; August 21; September 23, 26, 28; November 12, 13, 16; December 5, 26.

KEMPIS, THOMAS À (1380–1471), German religious writer, November 1.

KHAYYAM, OMAR (?–1123), Persian poet and philosopher, September 3.

KORAN, The, May 9; July 23.

KOSSUTH, LAJOS (1802–1894), Hungarian journalist and political activist, November 29.

KRISHNA, July 1.

LA BRUYÈRE, JEAN DE (1645–1696), French writer, March 5; April 20; June 25; August 7.

LAMARTINE, ALPHONSE MARIE LOUISE DE (1790–1869), French poet and statesman, June 20.

LAMENNAIS, F. ROBERT DE (1782–1854), French priest and writer, January 17; February 7; March 23; April 19; July 3; August 18, 24; December 18.

LAO-TZU (sixth century B.C.), Chinese philosopher, January 6, 19; February 9, 10, 22, 26; April 15; May 8; June 2, 8, 10, 27; July 17; September 13; October 4, 13; November 30; December 7, 13, 23.

LA ROCHEFOUCAULD, FRANÇOIS, 6TH DUC DE, (1613–1680), French writer, February 24.

LESSING, GOTTHOLD EPHRAIM (1729–1781), German philosopher, January 29; April 21; August 18; December 1.

LETURNO, December 29.

LICHTENBERG, GEORGE (1742–1799), German physicist and philosopher, April 1, 18, 26; May 5; July 9, 27; October 31; November 7, 8; December 27.

LUKE, SAINT, May 7.

LUTHER, MARTIN (1483–1546), German theologian, September 21.

MAIMONIDES, RABBI MOSES BEN (1135–1204), Jewish religious scholar, April 14.

MALORY, LUCY, American writer, journalist, editor of the journal *World's Advanced Thought,* February 5; April 20; May 4, 10, 22; June 3, 11, 25; July 1; August 12, 22; September 10; October 7, 12; December 7, 12.

MANU, a celebrated Hindu sage, the son of Brahma, January 29; June 8; August 23.

MARMONTEL, JEAN FRANÇOIS (1723–1799), French poet and novelist, May 30.

MARTIN, SAINT (c. 315–399), French churchman, a patron saint of France, April 9.

MARTINEAU, HARRIET (1802–1876), English writer, May 21; August 10; September 16.

MAUPASSANT, GUY DE (1850–1893), French novelist, July 6.

MAZZINI, GIUSEPPE (1805–1872), Italian patriot, head of the Italian struggle for independence, January 2; February 28, 29; March 17, 26; April 10, 12; June 19; July 3, 7; August 14, 16, 24; October 25; November 3, 16; December 18, 20, 22.

MENEDEMUS (350[?]–276 B.C.), Greek philosopher, May 23.

MICKIEWICZ, ADAM (1798–1855), Polish poet, September 27.

MILTON, JOHN (1608–1674), English poet, February 20.

MOHAMMED (570–632), the founder of Islam, March 15; May 6; July 11; December 11.

MOHK, GALSTON, June 17.

MOLINARI, GUSTAVE DE (1819–1912), Belgian economist, September 29.

MONTAIGNE, MICHEL DE (1533–1592), French essayist and philosopher, February 19; October 1.

MONTESQUIEU, CHARLES DE SECONDAT, BARON DE LA BRIDE (1689–1755), French philosopher, April 28; May 27.

NEWTON, HERBERT, November 10.

PALEY, WILLIAM (1743–1805), English theologian, February 23.

PAN, August 7.

PARKER, THEODORE (1810–1860), American Unitarian clergyman, April 8, 17; June 19; August 2; October 4.

PASCAL, BLAISE (1623–1662), French mathematician and theologian, February 12, 18; March 5, 14; April 11, 18, 26; July 1, 5; August 19; September 6, 14, 20, 22, 29; October 5; November 2, 9, 21; December 6, 17, 19, 21, 28, 31.

PERSIAN PROVERB (WISDOM), January 5, 13, 24, 27; May 1, 3, 14, 18.

PHILEMON (360[?]–263[?] B.C.), Greek playwright, September 3.

PLUTARCH (c. 46[?]–120[?]), Greek historian, August 15; September 19, 24.

PUBLILIUS SYRUS (first century A.D.), Roman poet, March 18.

PYTHAGORAS (sixth century B.C.), Greek philosopher, sage, mathematician, May 6; July 5; December 5.

RAFAEZSKY, ZANIZAD, April 11.

RICHE, CHARLES, September 29.

ROBERTSON, FREDERICK WILLIAM (1816–1853), English clergyman, July 28.

ROUSSEAU, JEAN JACQUES (1712–1778), French philosopher and writer, February 25; March 16; April 12, 26; May 15, 28; June 19; July 9; August 3, 15; October 23; December 6, 12.

RUSKIN, JOHN (1819–1900), English author and critic, January 3; February 3; March 7, 25; April 4, 15; May 13, 21, 22, 30; July 2, 11, 13; August 23, 31; September 7, 8, 9, 20, 23; November 26, 27; December 2, 10, 13, 18.

SAADI, OR SADI, MUSLIH-UD-DIN (c. 1184[?]–1291), Persian poet, January 4; February 26; March 3, 5, 15; April 5; July 16, 30; September 13; October 25.

SAID-BEN-HAMED, May 12.

SCHILLER, JOHANN CHRISTOPH FREDERICH VON (1759–1805), German dramatist and poet, January 29.

SCHOPENHAUER, ARTHUR (1788–1860), German philosopher, January 7, 9; February 21; May 6, 13; July 2, 12, 20; August 16; September 10, 15; October 3, 24; December 6, 12.

SENECA, LUCIUS ANNAEUS THE YOUNGER (c. 4 B.C.[?]–65 A.D.), Roman Stoic philosopher, January 1; March 3, 10, 20, 22; May 4; July 19; August 13, 20; September 18; October 8, 9, 16; November 14, 18, 26; December 12.

SHELLEY, PERCY BYSSHE (1792–1822), English poet, April 21.

SILESIUS, ANGELUS, February 22.

SKOVORODA, GREGORY (1722–1794), Ukrainian poet and philosopher, April 23.

SMILES, SAMUEL (1812–1904), Scottish writer and social reformer, April 4.

SOCRATES (469[?]–399 B.C.), Greek philosopher, January 23; June 25; August 20.

SOLON (638[?]–559 B.C.) Greek lawyer and poet, May 9; October 24.

SPENCER, HERBERT (1820–1903), English philosopher, September 17; November 14.

SPINOZA, BENEDICTUS (1632–1677), Dutch philosopher, June 5, 24; July 21; December 19.

STRAKHOV, FYODOR (1861–1923), Tolstoy's assistant and friend, April 12; September 10; October 27; December 22.

STRUVE, GUSTAV, December 26.

SUFI (a mystic branch of Islam) WISDOM, March 28; December 14.

TABLES OF THE BABIDS, a Muslim Sect from PERSIA, July 18

TALMUD, The, January 6, 11; February 10, 14, 18, 25; March 7, 8, 12, 18, 19, 28, 29, 31; April 7, 15; May 2, 5, 12, 21, 23; June 14, 15; July 15, 30, 31; August 3, 13; September 18; October 14, 19; November 17, 30; December 1, 11, 14, 24, 31.

THEOGNIS (?–541 B.C.), Greek poet, February 23.

THOREAU, HENRY DAVID (1817–1862), American essayist and poet, January 1, 9, 28; February 24; April 6; May 27; July 23; August 8, 27; September 14, 16, 25; November 22; December 12.

TOCQUEVILLE, ALEXIS CHARLES HENRI CLÉREL DE (1805–1859), French historian, March 21.

TORICLIDUS, September 22.

VIGNY, ALFRED VICTOR DE (1797–1863), French romantic writer, April 8.

VILLEMAIN, ABEL FRANÇOIS (1790–1870), French author and politician, May 7.

VOLTAIRE (FRANÇOIS MARIE AROUET) (1694–1778), French author, February 26; August 20.

VAUVENARGUES, LUC DE (1715–1747), French writer, April 13; August 9.

WARBURTON, WILLIAM (1698–1779), English churchman and writer, September 2.

WILKINS, GEORGE (1785–1865), English writer and clergyman, May 2.

XENOPHON (c. 434[?]–355 B.C.), Greek historian, January 25; July 9; September 23.

YATES, EDMUND, December 22.

ZIMMERMANN, JOHANN GEORG RITTER VON (1728–1795), Swiss writer and physician, June 20.

ZOROASTER (sixth century B.C.), founder of Zoroastrian religion, April 5; September 21.